UNVEILING THE MYSTERY OF THE CHURCH

UNVEILING THE MYSTERY OF THE CHURCH

Copyright 2012 by Rubye Edwards

All rights reserved. Written permission must be secured from the publisher to use or reproduce any part of this book, except for brief quotations in critical reviews or articles.

Printed in the United States of America

16   15   14   13   12   1   2   3   4   5

Library of Congress Control Number: 2011943209

ISBN: 978-1-937824-02-0

Cover design by Joey McNair at Defy Creative
Page design by LeAnna Massingille

Unless otherwise indicated, all scripture quotations are taken from the Holy Bible, King James Version, Cambridge, 1796.

PLUMBLINE MEDIA, LLC
415 BRIDGE STREET
FRANKLIN, TENNESSEE 37064
615-442-8582

WWW.PLUMBLINEMEDIA.NET

Words of such an undeserving one as I are inadequate to express gratitude to God for the unthinkable gift bestowed upon me of expressing his eternal word in writing. I thank God with all of my heart for his extraordinary revelations and pray that every reader will receive the wealth of unprecedented blessings which God intends for all.

CONTENTS

PREFACE   xi

Chapter One: PRAYER INTRODUCTION   1
Divine Provision • The Church's Specifics for Prayer • The Patriots Revered Prayer • Prayer for Discernment

Chapter Two: PRAYER FOR THE UNSAVED   11
Precedence • Unbelievers in Authority • Unbelievers with No Authority • Unbelievers with or without Authority • For Every Lost Soul

Chapter Three: PRAYER FOR AND WITH BELIEVERS   15
The Model Prayer • Watch, Pray, Repent • True Contrition • Transforming Prayer • Sincere Penitence • Seven Churches Admonished • Prayer for Church Restructuring • Love—A Requirement • Faith—A Requirement • The Word—A Requirement • Fleshly versus Spiritual • Paul's Prayer for Believers • Ultimate Requirements • Divine Help, Divine Results

Chapter Four: WORSHIP, PRAISE, THANKSGIVING   29
Blessing God Corporately • Praise and Adoration • All Creation Praises the Lord • The Saints' Praises to God • Thanksgiving • Highest Praise to the Most High God

Chapter Five: WHO IS GOD? 35
Acknowledging God • The Godhead is One • God the Father • God the Word • God the Holy Ghost • Sent to the World • Sent to Believers • One God, All in All • A Glimpse of Almighty God

Chapter Six: WHO ARE WE? 45
Creation of Man • The Fall of Man • The Temptation • Grave Consequences • Extreme Subtlety • Separations • Reconciliation • Salvation from Beginning to End • Divine Rescue with Covering • Winners versus Losers • After Eden—Cain and Abel, Violence and Wickedness • The Flood and Noah • Tower of Babel • Reprimand • Language Revisited • Abraham and Jacob (Israel) • The Promise Consummated • Division by Regeneration • The Transformation • The Promise Fulfilled • Salvation Foretold • Messiah Revealed • Acts of God • Moses, the Covenant, and the Ten Commandments • The Promise Precedes Law • New Covenant Established • Prophesies and Warnings • Wilderness Testings • Return to the Promised Land • Israel's Seventy-year Captivity and Return to Canaan

Chapter Seven: THE HOLY BETROTHAL AND MATRIMONY 71
John the Baptist • The Blessed Advent • Priceless Faith • Predestination, Birth, and Identity of the Church • Divine Purpose • Divine Grace • Believers Work and Labor with God • Provisions for the Body of Christ • Eight Pieces of Armor • The Mystery of the Body • Body Functions • Jesus Gives Ministering Gifts • God Assigns Ministering Gifts • Gifts and Work of the Holy Ghost • Bodily Activity or Inactivity • The Head of the Body • The Supreme Operator • The Administrator of the Church • The Foundation and Cornerstone • Apostles • Prophets • Evangelists • Pastors • Teachers • Divine Provision: Comforter and Helper • Call for Repentance • Repentance Equates Reversal • God's House of Prayer • Individual (Private) Prayer • Necessity of Suffering

Chapter Eight: ETERNAL LOVE   111
    Invincible Love • Love's Command • Genuine Love • Love's Tests • Virtual Love • Love is Eternal • A Fruit of the Spirit • Love Lost • Unsurpassed Love • God's Love Transcends Knowledge

Chapter Nine: THE MYSTERY—ONE CHURCH REVEALED IN THE LAST DAYS   121
    Hypothesis • The End of Time and Last Days • Who the Church Is Not • First Call • Remove the Obstacles • The Mystery Kingdom • Prepare for Visitation • The Azusa Awakening 1906–1924 • Return to the One Foundation • The Unveiled Mystery • Only One Way • Greater Works • Alpha and Omega of the Mystery

APPENDICES
    A. The Holy Spirit and the Gifts of the Spirit   149
    B. The Perfect Word of Truth   169

ABOUT THE AUTHOR   178

PREFACE

In all reverence and humility, I submit this observation relative to God's magnificent vision and revelation to the universal church of this generation. Beyond God's visitations of past church ages, God's message provides precise solutions for indispensable church revival and restoration. This action by God is, probably, the greatest manifestation of its kind given to the church in this manner for these last days. This is God's initiative alone.

God is exalted and glorified. Praise and gratitude belong to our holy God and our Savior. God's mercy, grace, and all things are provided to the body of Christ to accomplish all aspects of God's magnificent, preordained purposes and work in the earth for the good of all mankind in the final days.

Through these writings, sequel to the first book, God makes his intentions for the church renewal exceedingly plain and discernible. The results of this God-mandated revival will prove to be unprecedented and revolutionary. This unplanned and completely unexpected book evolved in a most miraculous way. During an extremely serious illness, which began in July 2001, undoubtedly, I prayed more intensely. This underscores my deep love for and longstanding commitment to prayer and study of the Word of God.

At some point, I noticed that my prayers had lengthened to about three hours and included every living human being. My first priority was and is prayer early each morning. During my extreme illness, it sometimes came later, depending on whether my condition required another emergency room visit or hospitalization. To this day, I have no recollection of how these prayers were so incredibly formed and organized and indelibly imprinted in my memory under such difficult circumstances. These prayers consist of Scripture read, heard, and memorized over the years and are prayed with unbelievable preciseness, consistency, and in sequence verbatim.

My desire was to share and engage other Christians in praying these prayers. In response to my endeavor, a second person suggested recording the prayers for preservation. At the conclusion of recording these prayers, to my surprise, titles and subtitles emerged. It became apparent that these writings illuminated the vision and revelation God gave resulting in the first book. This reinforced my continual expectation that the inevitable, God-initiated revival, revealed in 1984, could begin at any time. This knowledge is as fresh and vivid within me as when first given to me in October 1984.

This book is the coincidental sequel to the first book containing God's powerful vision and revelation to the church. That book, entitled *The Body of Jesus Christ*, was published in 1986. It details the impending great revival and restoration of the church. The first vision and revelation came during strange, prolonged, seemingly insurmountable troubles. This second book emerged from my most unusual suffering and deadly affliction. Believers are destined to follow in the steps of Jesus to the cross, though he alone suffered, died, and was resurrected supernaturally for all mankind.

The first book comprises the complete phenomenal message given by God in its original form. This sequel makes the vision unmistakably transparent. God has spoken again. In the most meticulous detail, God charters the course and shows the direct pathway to fulfillment of his command to the church at this eleventh hour. It is incumbent upon God's redeemed to hear him who speaks from heaven and has revealed the mystery of the church to this generation.

To read this book hurriedly, or with skepticism, or as a novel would be most regrettable. The greatest benefit to be obtained is to use a King James Holy Bible along with an Exhaustive Bible Concordance. As with the first book, this book contains the Word of God written in the language of the Bible. They are written in the first, second, and third person and refer to gender similarly as the Bible. The Word of God affirms his message by exposing the church's existing problems and providing exact solutions for correction. An expanded listing of Scripture references is provided.

Glory, praise, and honor to God for calling one so undeserving to write this sequel to make his revelation and vision unequivocally plain. The virulent sickness that I endured also caused the demise of many and resulted in this writing. Most important, I am deeply humbled as I recall the humanly incomprehensible choice Jesus made to endure ignominious suffering and death from pursuit by Herod to destroy him and even to the grave for everyone.

The church is to obey and respond to God's greatest visitation, I believe, since the birth of the church. God's phenomenal proclamation is current, prophetic, and climactic. It is sent to believers throughout the world. The end shall be the church reconstituted to conform to God's Word in holiness, power, and action predestined for these last days and end of time.

The sequel and the first book are one of a kind that have been written (obviously, the Bible excluded) proclaiming God's inevitable revival and restoration of the church. This church renewal illuminates and eliminates two prerequisite imperatives: (1) the church will finally know the exact major obstacle of which it must repent and (2) it complements and perfects ultimately the work of all previous revivals.

Chapter 1

PRAYER INTRODUCTION

And thou shalt make an altar to burn incense upon . . . And thou shalt put it before the vail that is by the ark of the testimony, before the mercy seat that is over the testimony [covenant], where I will meet with thee. And Aaron shall burn thereon sweet incense.
—**Exodus 30:1, 6–7**

And when he had taken the book, the four beasts and four and twenty elders fell down before the Lamb, having every one of them harps, and golden vials full of odours, which are the prayers of saints.
—**Revelation 5:8**

And another angel came and stood at the altar, having a golden censer; and there was given unto him much incense, that he should offer it with the prayers of all saints upon the golden altar which was before the throne. And the smoke of the incense, which came with the prayers of the saints, ascended up before God out of the angel's hand.
—**Revelation 8:3–4**

Having therefore, brethren, boldness to enter into the holiest by the blood of Jesus, By a new and living way, which he hath consecrated for us, through the veil, that is to say, his flesh.
—**Hebrews 10:19–20**

For mine house shall be called an house of prayer for all people.
—**Isaiah 56:7**

And they come to Jerusalem: and Jesus went into the temple, and began to cast out them that sold and bought in the temple, and overthrew the tables of the moneychangers, and the seats of them that sold doves; . . . And he taught, saying unto them, Is it not written, My house shall be called of all nations the house of prayer? but ye have made it a den of thieves.

—**Mark 11:15, 17**

DIVINE PROVISION

(1) Prayer was established and commanded by God for the servants and people of God. They built the golden altar of incense according to God's specification. The ordinance required the perpetual burning of sweet incense upon the golden altar, which was offered with the prayers of priests for themselves and for intercession and atonement of sins for all the people. Jesus observed the precedence of prayer and taught others to pray.

(2) Christians should know that there is no comparison, equivalent, or substitution for praying the Word of God. God's people are destroyed for lack of knowledge, which they reject. They are spiritually starved for refusing to hear God's Word.

God's great impending, unprecedented revival of the church is rooted in the church's sincere prayer and genuine repentance. Such prayer will correct the church's serious deficiencies and gross errors. This will be the beginning of the powerful, miraculous things awaiting the church.

(3) The greatest lack in the church today and the most imperative need is for prayer!

We need:
- a. more prayer,
- b. much prayer,
- c. prayer in the will of God,
- d. effectual, fervent prayer,

e. prayer in the faith, believing, and

   f. prayer with watching, fasting, and thanksgiving.

(4) We are instructed in the Word of God to:

   a. ask,

   b. pray without ceasing, and

   c. pray with confession, repentance, petitions, requests, supplications, and intercessions.

(5) We may pray in the morning, at noon, evening, the ninth hour, the third watch. We may pray at any time—day and night, with perseverance, persistence, importunity, without ceasing, continually, daily.

We are to continue instantly in prayer. We are to ask, seek, knock, receive, find, have access. There are also certain selected times of prayer mentioned in the Bible:

   a. Jesus prayed all night before he chose the twelve disciples.

   b. The disciples and the people went into the temple to pray at the hour of prayer. The ninth hour, which refers to the ninth hour of the day after dawn, is around 3:00 PM.

(6) When we pray, we may:

   a. bow down and kneel,

   b. stand, or

   c. pray with hands spread to heaven.

(7) The place of prayer may be:

   a. in the church or temple,

   b. in a solitary place,

   c. on the housetop,

   d. on the mountain top,

   e. in a house,

   f. in prison, or

   g. in a closet, in secret, privately.

(8) Let us thank God for:

   a. provision of prayer,

   b. power of prayer,

    c. privilege of prayer,
    d. blessings of prayer, and
    e. hearing and answering our prayers.

(9) Prayer, a divine foundation established by God, is the blessed means of communion and fellowship with God. We are invited to speak with God.

In times past, God spoke to the fathers by the prophets. Now, God speaks to us by his Son. We speak to God in the name of his Son, Jesus.

(10) God commanded that the golden altar of incense be built to burn sweet incense before the Lord perpetually throughout their generations. The altar was put before the veil, by the ark of the testimony, before the mercy seat. The priest burned holy anointing oil, pure incense of sweet spices. He prayed and made atonement for the people. At the golden altar of incense, God communed with Aaron from above the mercy seat between the two cherubims. Only the high priest was permitted once a year beyond the second veil into the holiest of all that housed the ark of the covenant, Aaron's rod, golden censer, and the golden pot of manna. The way into the holiest of all (salvation) was not manifested while the first tabernacle was standing. At the crucifixion of Jesus, the veil was split in two. When this happened, believers were granted boldness to enter into the holiest of all by the blood of Jesus. The new and living way into the holiest of all was consecrated by Jesus for us through the veil, that is to say, his flesh. By faith, believers are fully assured of access, having a true heart from a good conscience. Jesus has washed us with pure water. The ordinance of cleansing through the blood of bulls and goats was abolished. Remnants of past carnal customs were replaced upon receiving the teachings of Jesus. In the meantime, at the beginning of the New Testament era, Zacharias the priest continued the custom when he went into the temple to pray at the time, or hour, of incense. At that particular time, an angel of the Lord appeared to him and told him that his wife, Elizabeth, would have a son and to name him John, who was the messenger of Jesus.

THE CHURCH'S SPECIFICS FOR PRAYER

(11) Jesus taught us to pray that blessed, all-inclusive prayer, known as the Lord's Prayer, which is our model. Jesus also prayed a special prayer for believers.

The church is required to pray for everyone everywhere, to cover every living soul on the face of the earth, interceding and making supplications with thanksgiving.

(12) We are reminded in the book of Revelation that when the saints pray, our prayers are offered unto God upon the golden altar before the throne in bowls full of sweet fragrances.

(13) In the Old Testament and the New, God said that his house shall be called the house of prayer for all people.

As we pray, let us:
        a. humble ourselves and pray,
        b. strive together in prayer,
        c. pray the prayer of faith,
        d. pray with the Spirit,
        e. pray in the Spirit, and
        f. pray with understanding.

(14) As we pray for all souls everywhere, we are reminded of the blessed privilege also of praying and asking for anything, all things, and many things that are in accordance with God's will. This includes any and all specific persons, conditions, situations, or events.

(15) Why do believers need to pray? Prayer is indispensable. By the Spirit, believers have access to God through his Son. It produces intimacy with the Godhead, and it increases our belief, confidence, faith, and trust in God.

Prayer is for our benefit. We have great need to pray. God is holy, perfect, and eternal and has no need. God has all knowledge and knows what we need before we ask, whether spiritual, physical, or material. Our invisible God's marvelous provision of prayer is for us so that we also may know for a certainty that we are communicating with an omniscient God.

(16) Three ways of praying that are enormously effective and incredibly powerful are:

    a. fasting with prayer,

    b. praying in tongues, or

    c. two (or more) agreeing in prayer.

From the Word of God, the church learns how, when, where, why, and for whom to pray. Scripture is the source for answers, guidance, and direction. Believers are commanded to live by every word that proceeds out of the mouth of God. Specificly, the Scriptures are to be searched and followed in every situation and for every purpose; such as, sin, confession, repentance, and making the best choices and decisions. The outcome confirmed by the Word of God is unsurpassable.

In praying, we fulfill our obedience and faithfulness to God. We learn humility. Through prayer, we may know and understand God and the richness of his glory. We may learn God's will for our life and how to please him.

The value of prayer is incalculable. With much prayer according to God's will, believers and others may reap boundless, everlasting blessings. In the words of Tennyson, "more things are wrought by prayer than this world dreams of."

(17) God is present everywhere to act and work. When we pray, God hears and answers. As God commands, when we pray for every individual on the face of the earth, we know that God is performing his word faithfully in, through, and for people everywhere. God may or may not allow us to know of or see the fruit of our prayers, but we know that he is working throughout the world. Our prayers are pervasive. For instance, when we

hear of a catastrophic event or troubles or demise of any persons, we have the satisfaction of knowing that not one is or has been without our prayers for salvation, at the least. All those who yet need salvation, as well as all believers, continually receive prayer.

(18) The Word of God reminds believers that the end of all things is at hand. We are exhorted and commanded to be sober, to watch, and be aware of current happenings so that we may pray more effectively. When believers pray according to God's holy Word of instruction (given in considerable detail in this book) and ask anything according to his will, he hears us.

If we have confidence toward God, we know that he hears us and that we have the petitions we desire of him.

THE PATRIOTS REVERED PRAYER

(19) The Lord told Jeremiah to call unto him and he would answer and show him great and mighty things of which he had no prior knowledge. Great and mighty things await the church that obeys and prays according to the Word of God—things that have neither been previously heard of nor seen.

The Scriptures are filled with powerful prayers of outstanding holy patriots of God, psalmists, and a host of others. These are recorded for our example, guidance, and blessing. Saints prayed in sackcloth and ashes, with weeping, fasting, supplication, and with humility. Their petitions to God for answers, help, direction, protection, and deliverance reflected praise, worship, confession, repentance, and thanksgiving.

David's exemplary prayer concerning the house of God to be built by Solomon began with praise:

> Thine, O LORD, is the greatness, and the power, and the glory, and the victory, and the majesty: for all that is in the

heaven and in the earth is thine; . . . thou art exalted as head above all. Both riches and honour come of thee, and thou reignest over all; and in thine hand is power and might; . . . to make great, and to give strength unto all. Now therefore, our God, we thank thee, and praise thy glorious name (1 Chron. 29:11–13).

Hezekiah's prayer for deliverance from captivity, Daniel's prayers at his own peril, and Paul's prayers pertaining to the church are only a few examples of profuse, dynamic praying.

PRAYER FOR DISCERNMENT

(20) Christians who seek God, and pray faithfully and diligently according to the Word of God, prepare themselves to discern the great hidden mystery of the church. They will be in position to receive power for revolutionary change and unprecedented action by the church. God will teach the obedient believers to pray. This is to pray the Word of God, which is holy and unchangeable, the greatest and highest.

(21) Prayer is also a blessed means of reconciliation. Church restoration requires limitless united, contrite prayer saturated with confession, repentance, and resolve to do God's will. The church is the salt of the earth and light in the world, but is not of the world order. Increasingly, the world is expressing scorn, mockery, and rejection toward the church. To redeem itself of perceived apathy, the church should obey God and pray for all mankind. In the parable of the widow and the unjust judge, Jesus reminds us to persist in prayer. The church is to be nurtured, sustained, and empowered by continual exhaustive prayer. God commands and requires no less.

(22) The next two chapters on prayer conform to the Word and will of God. Praying these prayers, without doubt, will produce phenomenal spiritual biblical results for millions.

Scripture References

*Exodus 30:1–10;
   37:25–29; 39:38;
   40:1–6; 40:26–27*
Luke 1:9–10
Isaiah 56:7
Jeremiah 7:11
Matthew 21:13, 22
Mark 11:17
Luke 19:46
Matthew 6:9–15
John 17
1 Timothy 2:1–4
Ephesians 6:18
Revelation 5:8; 8:3–4
1 John 4:20–22
Jeremiah 33:3
Matthew 4:4
1 John 5:14–15
James 5:16
Mark 13:33

Colossians 4:2
1 Peter 4:7
Matthew 7:7–8
1 Thessalonians 5:17
1 John 1:9
Acts 6:4
Acts 2:46; 3:1; 10:30
Romans 12:12
Mark 11:23–24
Psalms 5:3; 55:17
Luke 6:12–13
Daniel 6:10
1 Kings 8:54
Mark 1:40
Acts 20:36
Ephesians 3:14
Psalm 141:2
Mark 1:35
Acts 10:9; 16:25
Matthew 6:6

2 Kings 4:33
Luke 8:51–54
Exodus 25:22
Hebrews 1:1–2
1 John 1:3
John 14:13–14
*Hebrews 9:3–14;
   10:19–22*
*Revelation 11:1; 14:18;
   16:7; 11:19*
2 Chronicles 7:14
Romans 15:30
1 Corinthians 14:15
1 John 3:23; 5:14
Matthew 14:13–14, 23
Ephesians 2:18
1 Chronicles 29:10–13
Luke 18:1–8
2 Kings 19:15–19

Chapter 2

PRAYER FOR THE UNSAVED

*I exhort therefore, that, first of all, supplications, prayers, intercessions, and giving of thanks, **be made for all men**; For kings, and for all that are in authority; that we may lead a quiet and peaceable life in all godliness and honesty. For this is good and acceptable in the sight of God our Saviour; Who will have all men to be saved, and to come unto the knowledge of the truth.*
	—**1 Timothy 2:1–4** (emphasis mine)

Then saith he unto his disciples, The harvest truly is plenteous, but the labourers are few; Pray ye therefore the Lord of the harvest, that he will send forth labourers into his harvest.
	—**Matthew 9:37–38**

PRECEDENCE

(1) Heavenly Father, we pray for every lost soul on the face of the earth, in obedience to your Word.

UNBELIEVERS IN AUTHORITY

(2) We pray for:
- a. everyone in authority from the most self-righteous to the least self-righteous; the most wicked, wealthy, wise, and powerful to the least;

     b. those who have been given the charge and responsibility, power and authority over all peoples of all the nations of the earth to: execute, govern, legislate, judge, and enforce law;
     c. those in charge of things pertaining to the environment, industry, manufacturing, trade, business, professions, and services; and
     d. those in authority who are parents, educators, in churches, in cults, the occult, and false religions (both Jews and Gentiles), and those who worship and serve idols.

UNBELIEVERS WITH NO AUTHORITY

(3) We pray for those who have no authority:
     a. babies, children, young people, students, workers, young, middle age and elderly persons;
     b. those who are confined or incarcerated;
     c. those who need food, clothing, shelter, and someone to help them, teach them, train them, and give them jobs;
     d. those who are oppressed and afflicted;
     e. those who are in great need and great danger;
     f. those who are despised, neglected, ignored, and considered to be expendable and disposable; and
     g. those who are in despair and have no hope.

UNBELIEVERS WITH OR WITHOUT AUTHORITY

(4) We pray for these whether they have authority or no authority:
     a. those who are the most vile, vicious, violent, and most wicked sinners on the face of the earth; and

    b. those who kill, steal and destroy mentally, physically, and emotionally through drugs, alcohol, tobacco, firearms, weapons—great and small—sexual assault, sexually transmitted diseases, pornography, rape, kidnapping, fraud, and extortion, whether by choice, decree, or consent.

FOR EVERY LOST SOUL

(5) For every lost soul on the face of the earth who is of the age of accountability and understanding, we pray:
    a. that they will have a dread and fear of death, hell and eternal damnation in the lake of fire more than ever before;
    b. that they will have the desire to be forgiven for their sins; and
    c. that they will desire the free gift of eternal life.

(6) To this end, we pray that they will allow the Holy Spirit to reprove them of sin, of righteousness, and of judgment.

We pray that they will desire to know the truth, to know who Jesus is, and what the Gospel means. We pray that they will prepare their hearts to receive the Gospel, to receive the truth, and to receive Jesus. For this cause, we pray that you would send forth laborers into the harvest field to preach the Gospel, heal the sick, raise the dead, cast out demons, and cleanse the leper.

We pray that the incorruptible seed, the Word of God, will fall on good ground and spring up into everlasting life. We thank you that you are not willing that any should perish but that all come to repentance.

(7) For every lost soul, Lord, we pray that you will:
    a. save them;
    b. baptize them with the Holy Ghost, and manifest through them spiritual gifts and ministry; and
    c. protect the innocent, comfort the bereaved, set the captives free, and incarcerate the wicked, we pray.

And we thank you, Father, in the name of Jesus, for hearing and answering prayer. Amen.

Scripture References

1 Timothy 2:1–4	Hebrews 9:27
John 3:13–18	2 Peter 3:9
Romans 3:22–26;	Psalm 16:11
10:6–21; 5:8–21	

Chapter 3

PRAYER FOR AND WITH BELIEVERS

***Praying always** with all prayer and supplication in the Spirit, and watching thereunto with all perseverance and supplication **for all saints**.*

—**Ephesians 6:18** (emphasis mine)

And when they were come in, they went up into an upper room, where abode both Peter, and James, and John, and Andrew, Philip, and Thomas, Bartholomew, and Matthew, James the son of Alphaeus, and Simon Zelotes, and Judas the brother of James. These all continued with one accord in prayer and supplication, with the women, and Mary the mother of Jesus, and with his brethren.

—**Acts 1:13–14**

Now when Solomon had made an end of praying, the fire came down from heaven, and consumed the burnt offering and the sacrifices; and the glory of the LORD filled the house. And the priests could not enter into the house of the LORD, because the glory of the LORD had filled the LORD's house.

—**2 Chronicles 7:1–2**

Confess your faults one to another, and pray for one another, that ye may be healed. The effectual fervent prayer of a righteous man availeth much.

—**James 5:16**

> *Again I say unto you, That if two of you shall **agree** on earth as touching [concerning or with respect to, not physical touching] any thing that they shall ask, it **shall** be done for them of my Father which is in heaven.*
>
> —**Matthew 18:19** (emphasis mine)

THE MODEL PRAYER

(1) As we pray for and with believers, we begin with the greatest prayer, the Lord's all-inclusive, divine model prayer:

> Our Father which art in heaven, Hallowed be thy name. Thy kingdom come. Thy will be done in earth, as it is in heaven. Give us this day our daily bread. And forgive us our debts, as we forgive our debtors. And lead us not into temptation, but deliver us from evil: for thine is the kingdom, and the power, and the glory, forever. Amen (Matt. 6:9–13).

Jesus teaches us to speak to God. As we do so, we acknowledge God's relationship to us as his children. We honor his name; ask and desire that his kingdom be established on earth—the Gospel of the kingdom having been preached in all the world, preceding the end of this age; that his will be done in earth as in heaven; we ask for food for sustenance of natural life and for help in maintaining our morality. We acknowledge that the kingdom, power, and glory belong only to God.

Jesus also explains to us that if we forgive men their trespasses, our heavenly Father will also forgive us; but if we do not forgive men their trespasses, neither will our heavenly Father forgive our trespasses.

(2) And so, Father, we ask you to help us to humble ourselves and pray and seek Thy face and turn from our wicked ways of lust of the flesh, lust of the eyes, and the pride of life. We have sinned and come short of your glory.

Help us to humble ourselves under the mighty hand of God and humble ourselves in the sight of the Lord.

Help us to cleanse our hands and purify our hearts and draw near unto you.

Help us to be afflicted, mourn, and weep and let our laughter be turned into mourning and our joy into heaviness, because we have not been the people you called us to be, and we have not done the work that you ordained us to do—not altogether as we should.

(3) Your Word reminds us that it is the goodness of God that leads us to repentance, and godly sorrow on our part works repentance unto salvation, but sorrow of the world works death. And he that covers his sins shall not prosper, but whoever confesses and forsakes his sins shall have mercy.

"If we say we have no sin, we deceive ourselves, and the truth is not in us. If we confess our sins, he is faithful and just to forgive us our sins and to cleanse us from all unrighteousness. If we say that we have not sinned, we make him a liar, and his word is not in us" (1 John 1:8–10).

WATCH, PRAY, REPENT

(4) Therefore, Father, we come boldly before your throne of grace that we may obtain mercy and find grace to help in time of need.

We need you to help us to acknowledge our sins, confess our sins, forsake our sins, and repent and return unto you and your Word from having a heart as an adamant stone, from being defiant against you, rebellious, impudent, obstinate, stiff-necked, stubborn, self-willed, self-determined, self-directed, self-contented, self-contained, self-sufficient, and self-sustained.

Help us to confess and repent for being carnal and carnal-minded, earthly and earthly-minded, fleshly and fleshly-minded, worldly and worldly-minded, insincere, hypocritical, and fraudulent, as Pharisees.

(5) Help us to remember the words of God and of Jesus that say that the day of the Lord shall come as a thief in the night; and Jesus says he

shall come as a thief in the night to give to every man according as their works shall be, whether they are good or evil; because our works shall be revealed by fire to see what sort it is, and some works shall be burned up.

Jesus admonishes us to watch and pray so that that day will not come upon us being unaware because we are asleep, and that day overtakes us, and that we will be ashamed at his coming.

But the Word tells us that that day shall not come except there come a falling away first. What if (and it appears as though) that falling away has already begun that the man of sin, the son of perdition, might be revealed.

(6) Father, help us to confess and repent, for the Scriptures tell us that in these last days of perilous times, we are lovers of our own selves and lovers of pleasure more than lovers of God. We are covetors, boasters, blasphemers, proud, despisers of those that are good, disobedient to parents, false accusers, incontinent, fierce, without natural affection, trucebreakers, traitors, heady, high-minded, unthankful, unholy, having a form of godliness, but denying the power thereof, from such we are to turn away. We are ever learning, but never able to come to the knowledge of the truth. Among those who do such things that have been named are those who creep into houses and lead captive silly women, who are laden with sins and carried away with diverse lusts.

(7) Help us to have ears to hear, for the Spirit speaks expressly that in the latter times some shall depart from the faith, giving heed to seducing spirits and doctrines of devils, speaking lies in hypocrisy, having their conscience seared with a hot iron. Evil men and seducers become worse and worse, being deceived and deceiving others.

Help us to repent, for the Word of God tells us that the time will come (it may have already come) when men will not endure sound doctrine, but heap to themselves teachers because they have itching ears; teachers that draw their ears away from the truth, and they are turned unto fables.

TRUE CONTRITION

(8) To counteract this condition, our Father, help us to desire truth in our inward parts; to hunger and thirst after righteousness; to strive to enter in at the straight gate, for wide is the gate and broad is the way that leads to destruction and many are those who go in at the wide gate—because straight is the gate and narrow is the way that lead unto life and there are few who find it.

(9) Jesus also says to us that not every one that says unto him Lord, Lord shall enter into the kingdom of heaven but they that do the will of his Father who is in heaven. Jesus says that in that day many will say unto him, have we not prophesied in thy name, and in thy name cast out devils, and in thy name done many wonderful works? Jesus says he will say unto these, I never knew you, depart from me you workers of iniquity.

TRANSFORMING PRAYER

(10) And now, Father, we need you to help us, the church today, the church of this present generation, to realize that we are in the valley of decision.

We are wandering in the wilderness. We are asleep. We have come to the crossroads and it is high time that we know the time, awake out of sleep, arise from the dead, and Christ will give us light so that we may make that 180-degree turn of repentance from sin, error, and disobedience, from repentance to righteousness, obedience, and holiness. To do this, Father, in Jesus' name, we ask you to help us to seek, desire, and strive earnestly, diligently, and urgently and see to it that our churches become houses of prayer for all people; second, that we become one; and third, that we become the church that is absolutely, totally, completely, and altogether on the foundation which Jesus Christ, himself, has laid;

and that foundation is the apostles and prophets, Jesus Christ, himself, being the chief cornerstone.

SINCERE PENITENCE

(11) Father, help us to abolish, abandon, cast down, deny, forsake, break up our fallow ground, root out, pluck up, throw down, and completely and utterly destroy forever all that we've built on that foundation of: gold, silver, precious stones, wood, hay, and stubble;

(12) Father, help us to abolish, abandon, cast down, deny, forsake, break up our fallow ground, root out, pluck up, throw down, and completely and utterly destroy forever all that we've built on that foundation of: the commandments of men; doctrines of men, error in doctrine, false doctrine, accepting and receiving and denying and rejecting portions of the Word of God as we see fit; attempting to revise the Word of God, which is impossible, because the Word of God is holy, eternal, and immutable.

Father, help us to repent for: corrupting the Word of God; handling the Word of God deceitfully; for straying away and deviating so far from the truth.

(13) Father, help us to abolish, abandon, cast down, deny, forsake, break up our fallow ground, root out, pluck up, throw down, and completely and utterly destroy forever all that we've built on that foundation of: dead ceremonies in our churches, dead rituals, dead programs, plans, practices, and exercises, dead works, and vain worship, for in vain do we worship God, teaching for doctrine the commandments of men. We draw near to God with our mouth and honor God with our lips, but our heart is far from God.

(14) Father, help us to abolish, abandon, cast down, deny, forsake, break up our fallow ground, root out, pluck up, throw down, and

completely and utterly destroy forever all that we've built on that foundation of: denominations of men; divisions of men; teachings of men; traditions of men.

(15) Heavenly Father, help us to have ears to hear what the Spirit is saying to the church that we are to hear God, repent and overcome.

SEVEN CHURCHES ADMONISHED

Help us to receive the admonition, exhortation, and counsel of Jesus in the revelation which God gave to him to show unto his servants; and Jesus sent and signified it by his angel to John, who wrote the revelation in a book and sent it to the seven churches in Asia. To every church Jesus said, I know thy works. To five of the churches Jesus said, hear, repent, and overcome. To two of the churches Jesus said, hear and overcome. (See Rev. 2 and 3.)

(16) Help us to have ears to hear, for Jesus said to one church: I know thy works. You are neither hot nor cold, but lukewarm. I desire that you were either hot or cold, and because you are lukewarm, I will spit you out of my mouth.

This same church said that they were rich and increased with good and had need of nothing; but Jesus said that they were wretched, miserable, poor, blind, and naked.

Jesus counseled this church to buy of him gold, tried in the fire, that they may be rich (truly rich); and white raiment that they may be clothed (clothed in robes of righteousness and holiness); to anoint their eyes with eye salve that they may see and be spiritually enlightened.

(17) In another church, Jesus said there are those who say they are apostles, but are not because they have been tried and found to be liars. Jesus said that this church had left their first love. They were admonished to repent from where they had fallen and do the first works or else he would come to them quickly and remove their candlestick out of its place.

PRAYER FOR CHURCH RESTRUCTURING

(18) Blessed Father, help us, the church of today, to repent and do the first works and discern, acknowledge, and receive into our churches the true apostles and prophets that the church may be built upon its true foundation of apostles and prophets, Jesus Christ, himself, being the chief cornerstone.

LOVE—A REQUIREMENT

(19) Father, help us to repent and return to our first love: to love God with all of our heart, soul, mind, and strength; to love our neighbor as ourselves; our brethren with a pure heart fervently; and to love our enemy.

And if we love God, we will obey God and keep his commandments, for when we obey God and keep his commandments, this is the proof that we love God; because these two are inseparable and mutually exclusive. We cannot have one without the other.

(20) The second commandment is like unto the first: that we are to love our neighbor as ourselves. If we do not love our neighbor whom we have seen, how can we love God whom we have not seen? And so when we love our neighbor, we love God; when we sin against our neighbor, we sin against God; because these two are inseparable and mutually exclusive. We cannot have one without the other.

FAITH—A REQUIREMENT

(21) We need you, Father, to help us to have belief, faith, trust, confidence, and hope in you and you alone, for without faith it is impossible to please God. Help us to have faith in God and live by the faith of the Son of God, who loved us and gave himself for us.

THE WORD—A REQUIREMENT

(22) Father, we ask you to please help us to love your Word, read your Word, study your Word, hear your Word, understand your Word, discern your Word, believe your Word, obey your Word, speak, preach, and teach your Word and live by every word that proceeds out of your mouth; but how can we live by every word if we do not know every word. Help us to study to show ourselves approved unto God, a workman that need not be ashamed, rightfully dividing the Word of truth. Adherence to the truth will absolutely remedy severe deficiencies, and God will intervene to help us discern, acknowledge, and receive into our churches the true teachers, teachers whom Jesus has given the ministering gift of teaching; teachers whom God has set in the church third after the apostles and prophets.

FLESHLY VERSUS SPIRITUAL

(23) We need you, Father, to help us to: be spiritual, be in the Spirit, be after the Spirit, follow after the Spirit, and be filled with the Spirit. Help us to be: led of the Spirit, live in the Spirit, love in the Spirit, mind the things of the Spirit, be spiritually minded, pray in the Spirit, preach in the Spirit, sing in the Spirit, speak in the Spirit, teach in the Spirit, walk in the Spirit, walk after the Spirit, and worship you in spirit and in truth.

That which is born of the flesh is flesh; that which is born of the Spirit is spirit. Thank you, Father, that we are not in the flesh, but in the Spirit, if the Spirit of God dwells in us. Whoever does not have the Spirit of Christ is none of his. If Christ is in us, the body is dead because of sin, but the Spirit is life because of righteousness. And if the Spirit of him that raised Jesus from the dead dwells in us, he that raised up Christ from the dead shall also quicken our mortal bodies by his Spirit that dwells in us.

PAUL'S PRAYER FOR BELIEVERS

(24) To help us further, Father, we pray the prayers that Paul prayed for the saints of the churches of the Ephesians, the Philippians, and the Colossians.

The Ephesians: Father, please give us the spirit of wisdom and revelation in the knowledge of thee; the eyes of our understanding being enlightened that we may know what is the hope of your calling and what is the riches of the glory of your inheritance in the saints. And what is the exceeding greatness of your power toward us who believe, according to the working of your mighty power which you wrought in Christ when you raised him from the dead and set him at your own right hand in heavenly places, far above all principality, and power, and might and dominion, and every name that is named, not only in this world, but also in that which is to come. And has put all things under his feet, and gave him to be the head over all things to the church, which is his body, the fullness of him that fills all in all.

Please grant us according to the riches of your glory to be strengthened with might by thy Spirit in our inner man that Christ may dwell in our hearts by faith that we, being rooted and grounded in love, may be able to comprehend with all saints what is the breadth and length and depth and height and to know the love of Christ which passes knowledge, that we may be filled with all the fullness of God. (See Eph. 1:17–23; 3:16–19.)

The Philippians: We request with joy, fellowship with the saints in the Gospel. And we would add these: that we would be one, in one accord, in agreement, one in Christ, one in the body of Christ, one in faith, one in holiness, one in humility, one in love, one in mind, one in prayer, one in praise, one in spirit, one in truth, one in the Word, one in worship, one in togetherness and unity in Jesus' name.

We pray as Paul prayed that our love may abound yet more and more in knowledge and in all judgment that we may approve things that are excellent and that we may be sincere and without offense until the day of

Christ; being filled with the fruits of righteousness which are by Jesus Christ, unto the glory and praise of God. (See Phil. 1:4–11.)

The Colossians: We pray and desire that we might be filled with the knowledge of your will in all wisdom and spiritual understanding that we might walk worthy of the Lord unto all pleasing, being fruitful in every good work, and increasing in the knowledge of God; strengthened with all might, according to your glorious power, unto all patience and long-suffering with joyfulness; giving thanks unto the Father, which has made us meet to be partakers of the inheritance of the saints in light; who has delivered us from the power of darkness, and has translated us into the kingdom of his dear Son; in whom we have redemption through his blood, even the forgiveness of sins. (See Col. 1:9–14.)

ULTIMATE REQUIREMENTS

(25) Now Father, we ask you to help us to do the extremely hard and very difficult things that are required of us, and that is to: hate our life, lose our life, hate mammon, and forsake all and follow Jesus. Help us to receive the admonition, exhortation, and counsel of Jesus: that any man or woman who comes to him and does not hate his father, mother, husband, wife, children, brothers, sisters, and his own life also, he cannot be his disciple.

And whoever does not bear his cross and come after Jesus cannot be his disciple. Whoever among us who does not forsake all that he has he cannot be his disciple. No man can serve two masters: for either he will hate the one and love the other; or else he will hold to the one and despise the other. We cannot serve God and mammon. Help us to remember the plight of the rich young ruler, who came to Jesus and asked what he should do to inherit eternal life. When Jesus offered him true riches and the free gift of eternal life, he was grieved and went away sorrowful, because he had great riches. He was deceived by the riches of this world, which are counterfeit and false, can be moth-eaten, rust away, and stolen, and because they are corruptible and temporal shall be burned up when the world is on fire.

(26) We thank you, Father, that you have greater riches for us than the riches of this world, that you will help us to be all that you called us to be and do all that you have ordained us to do, as we commit our way unto you, submit ourselves unto you, subject ourselves unto you, yield unto you, and present our bodies a living sacrifice, holy, acceptable unto you, which is our reasonable service. And we are not to be conformed to this world, but be transformed by the renewing of our mind that we may prove that good and acceptable and perfect will of God.

Father, we ask you to help us to know you, know your voice, hear your voice, know your will, and do your will and your will alone. We pray that our dread and fear will be of you; our desire will be to you, and that we will cleave to you all the days of our lives.

DIVINE HELP, DIVINE RESULTS

(27) And now, Father, before we conclude our prayers, requests and petitions, we thank you and praise you, bless you, honor you, worship you, and love you for all that you have done, all that you are doing, and all that you are going to do in our lives.

We thank you for the provision of prayer, the privilege of prayer, the power of prayer, the blessings of prayer, and for hearing and answering prayer.

(28) Thank you for your visitation to the church at this present hour. Thank you for your intervention into the life of the church. Thank you for your initiative to revive, renew, and restore the church to be the church that is on its true foundation: structured, operating, and functioning according to your holy desire, design, plan, purpose, will, Word, and work before the foundation of the world.

And Father, help us not to have a drawback spirit and resist the Spirit, grieve the Spirit, and quench the Spirit. Help us to neither doubt nor fear, but have faith; for you are the God of all grace who gives us grace; the God of peace who gives us peace that passes all understanding; you work in us, both to will and to do of your good pleasure. And you are well able, because you have all power, and there is no power but the power of God.

And now, Father, we close our prayers with the conclusion of Peter and the benedictions to the Hebrews and Ephesians:

> But the God of all grace, who hath called us unto his eternal glory by Christ Jesus, after that ye have suffered a while, make you perfect, stablish, strengthen, settle you. To him be glory and dominion for ever and ever. Amen (1 Peter 5:10–11).
>
> Now the God of peace, that brought again from the dead our Lord Jesus, that great shepherd of the sheep, through the blood of the everlasting covenant, Make you perfect in every good work to do his will, working in you that which is wellpleasing in his sight, through Jesus Christ; to whom be glory for ever and ever. Amen (Heb. 13:20–21).
>
> Now unto him that is able to do exceeding abundantly above all that we ask or think, according to the power [your power] that worketh in us, Unto him be glory in the church by Christ Jesus throughout all ages, world without end. Amen (Eph. 3:20–21).
>
> We thank you in the name of Jesus for hearing and answering prayer.

Scripture Reference:

Matthew 6:9–15
Ephesians 6:18
James 4:7–10
1 John 2:15–16
2 Chronicles 7:14
2 Corinthians 7:10
Proverbs 28:13
1 John 1:8–10
Hebrews 4:16
Zechariah 7:12
Ezekiel 2:4
Romans 8:5–8
Luke 11:44
1 Corinthians 6:8
Titus 2:12
Philippians 3:19
2 Peter 3:10
1 Thessalonians 5:2–4
Matthew 16:27
Mark 13:36
1 Corinthians 3:13–15
Luke 21:34
1 John 2:28
Revelation 3:31, 16:15
2 Thessalonians 2:3
2 Timothy 3
1 Timothy 4:1
2 Timothy 4:3–4

Psalm 51:6
Matthew 5:6; 7:13–14, 21–23
Luke 19:46
Isaiah 56:7
John 17:11, 21
1 Peter 2:6
1 Corinthians 3:10–12
1 Timothy 1:17
Hebrews 6:17
1 Peter 1:23, 25
Romans 1:20
2 Corinthians 2:17; 4:2
Hebrews 6:1
Matthew 15:8–9
1 Corinthians 1:10–13; 3:3
Revelation 2
Ephesians 2:20–22
Matthew 22:37–39
John 13:34–35
1 John 2:7–11
Hebrews 11:6
Galatians 2:20
Matthew 28:19–20; 4:4
2 Timothy 2:15
John 24:45
Luke 8:21
Ephesians 4:11

1 Corinthians 12:28
Romans 8:1–11
Ephesians 1:16–23; 3:14–21
Philippians 1:3–11
Colossians 1:9–14
Matthew 6:24; 12:25
Mark 8:35
Luke 14:26; 16:13
Matthew 16:25
John 12:25
Luke 14:26–27, 33; 16:13
Romans 12:1–2
Ephesians 1:4–5; 9–12
1 Thessalonians 5:19
Ephesians 4:30
Acts 7:51
Hebrews 12:25–29
Romans 13:1
1 Peter 5:10–11
Hebrews 13:20–21
Ephesians 3:20–21
1 Peter 5:10–11
Hebrews 13:20–21
Ephesians 3:20–21
Colossians 3:17

Chapter 4

WORSHIP, PRAISE, THANKSGIVING

*But the hour cometh, and now is, when the true worshippers shall worship the Father in spirit and in truth: for the Father **seeketh** such to worship him.*

—**John 4:23** (emphasis mine)

Oh that men would praise the LORD for his goodness, and for his wonderful works to the children of men!

—**Psalm 107:8**

O give thanks unto the LORD, for he is good: for his mercy endureth forever.

—**Psalm 107:1**

Let them exalt him also in the congregation of the people, and praise him in the assembly of the elders.

—**Psalm 107:32**

BLESSING GOD CORPORATELY

(1) "And David said to all the congregation, Now bless the LORD your God. And all the congregation blessed the LORD God of their fathers, and bowed down their heads, and worshipped the LORD, and the king." Note that they also worshipped king David, who led them in worship and praise.

PRAISE AND ADORATION

(2) We kneel, bless God (as an act of adoration) abundantly; praise, give thanks. We speak well of (thank or invoke a benediction upon, prosper, bless, praise) God.

With the psalmist, we also affirm: "Bless the Lord, O my soul: and all that is within me, bless his holy name. I will bless the Lord at all times; his praise shall continually be in my mouth. Every day will I bless thee; and I will praise thy name forever and ever."

(3) "Great is the Lord, and greatly to be praised; and his greatness is unsearchable. My mouth shall speak the praise of the Lord. Praise ye the Lord. Praise the Lord, O my soul."

"While I live, will I praise the Lord: I will sing praises unto my God while I have my being."

Almighty, Eternal God, and our Father, we love you. We worship you. We praise you. We thank you. We honor you. We bless you.

We praise and worship you Almighty, Everlasting God now and forever, because you are One. You are: God, our heavenly Father; God, the Word, Jesus Christ our Lord and Saviour; and God the Holy Ghost, the Holy Spirit, Spirit of God, Spirit of Christ.

We worship and praise you for your love, your grace, your faithfulness, your goodness, your lovingkindness and tender mercies, your longsuffering, patience, pity, and compassion. We exalt thee. We extol thee. We glorify and magnify your holy name. We admire you and we adore you. You are Majestic. You are glorious. You are holy. You alone are worthy of all praise and glory.

ALL CREATION PRAISES THE LORD

(4) Praise the Lord:
> From the heavens;
> In the heights;

All his angels, all his hosts;
Sun, moon, stars;
Heaven of heavens;
Waters above the heavens.

Praise the Lord from the earth; dragons, and all deeps; fire, hail, snow, vapors, stormy winds, mountains, hills, trees; beasts, cattle, creeping things, flying fowl.

Praise the Lord:
Kings of the earth;
All people, princes, judges;
Young men, maidens;
Old men and children.

THE SAINTS' PRAISES TO GOD

(5) Praise the Lord all the people, saints of God, in his Sanctuary and declare:
His name alone is excellent.
His glory is above the earth and heaven.
He exalts the horn (strength) of his people, the praise of all his saints
Praise ye the Lord.

(6) Praise ye the Lord. Praise God:
In the firmament of his power;
For his mighty acts;
According to his excellent greatness.

(7) Praise him:
With the sound of the trumpet;
With the psaltery and harp;

With the timbrel and dance;
With the stringed instruments and organs;
Upon the loud cymbal, high sounding cymbal.
Let everything that hath breath praise the Lord.
Praise (hallelujah) to the Lord.

Solomon's prayers, supplications, and answers from God brought down fire, and the glory of God filled the house. When the people saw this sight, they bowed with their faces to the ground upon the pavement and worshipped and praised the Lord.

Some church assemblies have experienced the rapture of the wondrous glory of God similarly as the saints of the Old Testament times. When their sounds went up to God in singing, playing musical instruments, and lifting up their voices praising and thanking God, the house where they were gathered was filled with a cloud, the glory of God. The priests could not minister because of the glory of the Lord that filled the house.

THANKSGIVING

(8) Give thanks unto the Lord, for he is good; for his mercy endures forever. Thank you, heavenly Father, for your great love, great grace, great faithfulness, great lovingkindness, and tender mercies, great longsuffering and patience, great pity, great compassion.

Thank you for great salvation, redemption, and forgiveness of sin.
Thank you for all spiritual blessings in heavenly places in Christ Jesus.
Thank you for your holy, eternal word, the Holy Scripture, the written Word of God.
Thank you for all things that pertain unto life and godliness;
Thank you for your excellent greatness;
Thank you for your mighty acts;
Thank you for your wonderful works to the children of men.

(9) Many psalmists expressed immense thanksgiving and gratitude to God. These are for our example, blessing, and edification, and we thank God for them. Psalm 103 is a superb culmination of God's extraordinary blessings enjoyed by all believers that should be acknowledged unto God daily.

HIGHEST PRAISE TO THE MOST HIGH GOD

(10) "Thine, O LORD, is the greatness, and the power, and the glory, and the victory, and the majesty: for all that is in the heaven and in the earth is thine; thine is the kingdom, O LORD, and thou art exalted as head above all" (1 Chron. 29:11).

"For thine is the kingdom, and the power, and the glory forever, Amen" (Matt. 6:13).

"For there is no power but of God: the powers that be are ordained of God" (Rom. 13:1).

An exposition of God's omnipotency is shown in Job 36:22, 37–41, and 42:1–6. This shows man's struggle to grasp God's infinite greatness and power.

(11) There is reciprocity in worship and praise. Those who sincerely, profusely give praise, worship, adoration, and thanksgiving to God will certainly experience a most amazing, fervent spiritual response. Believers may sense an awareness also of God's presence, through reading, hearing, and meditating on his Word, through service, and through answer to prayer. It is so wonderfully refreshing to be able to experience the divine presence of God within and to see the glorious manifestation of his presence without.

"By him therefore let us offer the sacrifice of praise to God continually, that is, the fruit of our lips, giving thanks to his name" (Heb. 13:15).

(12) When we regularly offer high praises, worship, and thanksgiving to God, some may think that they have exhausted appropriate words of their

vocabulary. Let there be no surprise when such praise is so ecstatic that this joy transcends into speaking praises to God in an unknown language neither learned nor understood, but is manifested by the Holy Spirit.

All things were created for your pleasure, Lord God Almighty. Worthy is the Lamb of God. Thine, O Lord, is the kingdom, the power, and the glory, dominion, excellency, goodness, greatness, holiness, majesty, might, splendor, strength, wisdom, knowledge, understanding, honor, riches, and blessings, forever and ever. Amen.

Praising God is a most blissful and glorious experience. Praise and worship take our mind off ourselves and our natural state and focus it in the realm of the spiritual. Our worship of God begins here and now, unceasingly, with super abundant thanksgiving and praise for no other reason than our love of God compels us. God alone is worthy of all praise. When we get to heaven and come before our God, there will be no less desire than to praise God continually and eternally.

(13) The word *holy*, transcends our natural understanding. We will rejoice greatly, however, as we experience the glory that words bring to our spirit when we worship, praise, and adore the Holy One.

(14) "And the four beasts had each of them six wings about him; and they were full of eyes within: and they rest not day and night, saying, Holy, holy, holy, Lord God Almighty, which was, and is, and is to come" (Rev. 4:8).

The twenty-four elders fall down before God and cast their crowns before his throne just at the hearing of the word *holy*. Amen.

Scripture References:

1 Chronicles 29:20	*John 1:1*	*1 Kings 8:10–12*
Psalm 103:1–14	*2 Peter 1:20–21*	*2 Chronicles 7:1–3*
2 Chronicles 5; 7	*2 Timothy 3:16*	*Leviticus 9:6*
Psalms 34:1–3; 145:2–3,	*Revelation 19:13*	*Hebrews 13:15*
21; 146:1–2; 148; 150;	*2 Peter 1:3*	*Psalm 149:6*
105:1, 106:1, 107:1	*1 Chronicles 29:11*	*Revelation 5:12; 7:12–13;*
Ephesians 1:3	*Exodus 16:10; 40:34*	*4:8–11*

Chapter 5

WHO IS GOD?

And God said unto Moses, I AM THAT I AM: and he said, Thus shalt thou say unto the children of Israel, I AM hath sent me unto you.

—**Exodus 3:14**

In the beginning was the Word, and the Word was with God, and the Word was God.

—**John 1:1**

And I will pray the Father, and he shall send you another Comforter, that he may abide with you for ever.

—**John 14:16**

For there are three that bear record in heaven, **the Father, the Word, and the Holy Ghost: and these three are one.**

—**1 John 5:7** (emphasis mine)

Now there are diversities of **gifts**, *but the same Spirit. And there are differences of* **administrations**, *but the same Lord. And there are diversities of* **operations**, *but it is the same God which worketh all in all.*

—**1 Corinthians 12:4–6** (emphasis mine)

Can any hide himself in secret places that I shall not see him? saith the L{\scriptsize ORD}. *Do not I fill heaven and earth? saith the* L{\scriptsize ORD}.

—**Jeremiah 23:24**

ACKNOWLEDGING GOD

(1) God is eternal existence. God is from everlasting to everlasting. God, the I Am that I Am, is self-existent. He permeates all that exists. God's name alone is Jehovah. God Almighty is the Lord. God is Alpha and Omega.

THE GODHEAD IS ONE

(2) You are:
>God the Father,
>God the Word, and
>God the Holy Ghost.

You are:
>One God, three persons, co-equal.
>There are many gods, but only one true God.
>And there is no other God beside you;
>No other God like unto you;
>No other God with you;
>No other deity or divine being;
>No trinity or three united to make one.
>You are God.

You are:
>Omnipotent—all powerful;
>Omniscient—all knowing; and
>Omnipresent—everywhere present.

GOD THE FATHER

(3) You are God and Father of our Lord and Saviour Jesus Christ. You are the lofty One that inhabits eternity whose name is Holy; you dwell in the high and holy place; Heaven is your throne; earth is your footstool.

It is you who sits on the circle of the earth, and the inhabitants of the earth are as grasshoppers.

You are the Lord God of hosts.

The earth is the Lord's and the fullness thereof, the world and they that dwell therein.

You are God, the Operator of many diverse operations, and you operate and work all things after the counsel of your own will.

You, God, only are wise and have all wisdom and all knowledge and your understanding is infinite.

You are God, the Judge of all; and you are the Avenger. Vengeance belongs to God alone. Your judgments are unsearchable, and your ways are past finding out.

You are God who is above all and through all, for in thee we all live and move and have our being, even so-called atheists and agnostics.

You, God, are in us all, who have been saved by the blood of Jesus, born of the Spirit, and translated into the kingdom of thy dear Son.

All things are of thee and through thee and to thee to whom be glory and dominion forever and ever.

GOD THE WORD

(4) You are God the Word, God Incarnate.

> You are the Word made flesh, who dwelled among men.
> You are the only begotten Son of God.
> You are the heir of all things.
> You are the only Lord and Saviour, Redeemer, Jesus Christ, the Messiah.
> You are the firstborn of every creature.
> You are Emmanuel, God with us, Son of Man.
> You are the Lamb of God slain before the foundation of the world.
> You are the first begotten of the dead.

You are the firstborn from the dead.
You are the resurrection and the life.
You are wonderful, Counselor, the mighty God, everlasting Father,
Prince of Peace, Prince of the kings of the earth.
You are the Rose of Sharon and lily of the valleys.
You are the bright and morning star.
You are the Lion of the tribe of Judah.
You are a rod out of the stem of Jesse.
You are the root and offspring of David.
You are the branch.
You are King of kings and Lord of lords.

(5) You were sent by God the Father and you came into the world to save the world from sin and to save your people from their sins. You are the only Lord and Saviour, Master, Redeemer.

There is no other name under heaven given whereby we must be saved.

You are the only mediator between God and men, the man Christ Jesus.

You are the great Intercessor.

You are the way, the truth, and the life. No one comes to the Father except by you.

You are the Light of the world, who gives light to everyone who comes into the world, that all may come to the Light, believe in you, and be saved.

(6) To the believers you are not only our Lord and Saviour, Master, and Redeemer, but you are the Administrator and head of the church, which is your body.

There are differences of administrations, but you are the one Lord of all and over all administrations.

To the body of Christ, you are the Bridegroom of the bride;

You are the elder brother of the sons and daughters of God;

You are the Apostle, the Prophet, the Evangelist, the Pastor (the Great Shepherd, the Chief Shepherd, the Great High Priest), and the Teacher.

To the members of the body of Christ you gave the ministering gifts of apostle, prophet, evangelist, pastor, and teacher.

You are also our advocate with the Father.

You are our intercessor.

You are our leader, and we are to follow your steps.

You are our baptizer with the Holy Ghost.

You are our healer.

You are our King.

Jesus, the Word, is the Ancient of days. He is from everlasting—before he created light and called it day. On the Isle of Patmos, Jesus showed John a vision of himself having hairs as white like wool and as white as snow. His eyes were as a flame of fire and his feet were like fine brass.

Scripture References:

John 1:1–3	Psalm 147:5	1 Corinthians 12:14,
Colossians 1:5	Acts 17:28	27–28
Hebrews 1:5; 1:2	Ecclesiastes 3:19–21, 12:7	Ephesians 1:22–23
John 1:14	2 Corinthians 5:4–8	1 Corinthians 12:5
Revelation 19:13, 16	John 3:16–17; 4:42;	Romans 12:4–16
Matthew 1:23; 12:8	12:47	John 3:29
Colossians 1:15	1 John 4:14	Revelation 19:7–9; 21:2, 9
John 1:29; 4:25	John 1:29	Matthew 25:1
Revelation 1:5, 8	1 Timothy 1:15	Hebrews 3:15, 6:20
Colossians 1:18	Matthew 1:21	Isaiah 61:1
Isaiah 9:6	Hebrews 9:26; 10:10–12	Matthew 4:17, 11:1, 21:23
Song of Solomon 2:1	Acts 4:12	Ephesians 4:7–16
Revelation 22:16; 5:5	1 Timothy 2:5	Psalm 83:18
Isaiah 11:1	Hebrews 9:15	Exodus 3:13–14; 6:2–3
Zechariah 3:18; 6:12	Romans 8:26	Isaiah 12:2; 26:4
Ephesians 1:11	Hebrews 7:25	Jeremiah 10:16; 50:34
Hebrews 12:23	Isaiah 53:12	Daniel 7:9
Romans 11:33	John 14:6; 1:9; 8:12	Psalm 90:2
Jeremiah 51:15	Luke 2:11	Revelation 1:14
1 Timothy 1:17	Acts 10:36	
Jude 25	Romans 3:24	

GOD THE HOLY GHOST

(7) You are God the Holy Ghost, the Holy Spirit, the Spirit of God, the Spirit of Christ.

You are the Spirit of grace, the Spirit of life, the Spirit of truth.

SENT TO THE WORLD

(8) You were sent by God the Father and you came into the world to reprove the world of sin, of righteousness, and of judgment, to include both sinners and believers.

SENT TO THE BELIEVERS

(9) You were sent by God the Father and you came into the world to indwell the believers.

You baptize all believers into one body, the body of Christ.

You give to the members of the body of Christ nine spiritual gifts.

You divide these gifts among believers giving to each one according to your will.

You manifest and work these gifts in and through the members of the body of Christ so that the entire body of Christ may prosper with these spiritual gifts.

You are also our Comforter, our Guide, Helper, Intercessor, Leader, Reminder, Revelator, and Teacher.

Scripture References:

Hebrews 10:29	*John 14:26; 14:17*	*John 16:13*
Romans 8:2	*1 Corinthians 12:13; 12:4;*	*Romans 8:26; 8:14*
John 16:8–11	*12:11; 12:7*	*John 15:26*
Luke 24:49		

ONE GOD, ALL IN ALL

(10) You are one God and three persons. You are Alpha and Omega, the first and the last, the beginning and the ending, who was, and is, and is to come.

(11) You are the Creator and Maker of all things in heaven and in earth, both visible and invisible, whether they are thrones or dominions, principalities or powers, persons, places, or things. All things were created by Jesus and for Jesus and without Jesus nothing was made that was made. Jesus is and was before all things, and by Jesus all things consist. Jesus upholds all things by the word of his power.

As God the Almighty, you have all strength, all might, all authority, all power, and all dominion over all of creation. You are victorious and triumphant, who can do anything and everything, for nothing is impossible with God.

You are God eternal, everlasting, invisible, immortal, unchangeable.

You are holy, perfect, righteous, divine, majestic, glorious.

You are love. You are light. You are life. You are Spirit. Thine is the kingdom, the power, and the glory. Thine also is dominion, excellency, goodness, greatness, holiness, magnificence, majesty, might, strength, wisdom, knowledge, understanding, honor, riches, and blessings, forever. Amen.

A GLIMPSE OF ALMIGHTY GOD

(12) The following biblical account of the exceptional interaction between God, Job, and the enemy, Satan, is certainly worth citing.

God praised Job, whom he said was the most upright and perfect man and none in the earth was like him. It was through Job's horrifying experience that God would reveal himself to Job and show his sovereign power to Satan. God accepted the challenge Satan posed—that Job would curse God if God would take away his blessed work and enormous substance. To prove the contrary, God permitted Satan to destroy Job's children and physically afflict him. In all this, Job did not sin, nor did he charge God foolishly. Instead, he fell to the ground in submission and worshipped God.

Job's three friends heard of his adversities and they came to mourn and comfort him. Instead, they ineptly disputed with Job and harshly judged him, because they were infuriated by Job's replies. After Job's miserable comforters ceased speaking to him, Elihu, who had been listening to the discourse, also became angry in his spirit against Job. He accused Job of being righteous in his own eyes in that he justified himself rather than God. Elihu's anger was also directed toward Job's three friends; because, he said, they had no answer yet condemned Job.

Job had related to his friends how he had lived an upright life. He shunned evil. He was careful not to lust neither according to the flesh nor what his eyes looked upon.

He gave to the poor. Job lamented that the very principles he had been so careful to uphold seemed to have come back to mock him.

After all four visitors had ceased speaking, God appeared to Job out of the whirlwind and said that his three friends' words were without knowledge. God's questions demanded of Job answers that produced in him contrite introspection. Job began to learn more about God in light of his own deficiencies, which he acknowledged. He recollected, among other things, God's eternal existence, power, knowledge, dominion, perfection, and holiness. God asked Job profound questions such as, who fastened the foundation of the earth, measured boundaries and depths of the seas, or had seen the doors of the shadow of death?

(13) God described how his matchless power cannot be remotely compared with the great terrible strengths of the most fearless of beasts. The wild horse, God said, swallows the ground with fierceness and rage, and he mocks at fear. The behemoth is chief of the ways of God. He drinks up a river and trust that he can draw up the river Jordan into his mouth.

The intrepid leviathan with his comely proportions, says the Almighty, is so fierce that none dare stir him up. Who can open the doors of his face? His scales are his pride, shut up as a seal so closely stuck together that not even air can come between them. The flakes of his flesh are firm and joined together so that they cannot be moved. His bones are like bars of iron. He esteems iron as straw, and there is none on earth like him who is made without fear, who casts down those even at the sight of him. The question to mankind then is: Who, therefore, is able to approach unto the Almighty God or discover or move him?

(14) It is required of believers to truly know God, rather than vaguely know about him. Believers may know God more intimately, and this often comes through strange trials and intense sufferings. Job cried out in agony, that he might find God and even come to his seat. Job said, nevertheless, he had kept God's commandments, that God had known his ways, and that when he had been tried, he would come forth as gold. God revives the heart of those who are of a humble and contrite spirit. The Lord says you shall seek Me, and find Me when you shall search for Me with all your heart and soul, and I will be found of you.

(15) When Job admitted his shortcomings, God's grace enabled him to know God—not just by hearing about him, but by truly spiritually seeing he who is invisible. Forgiveness followed true repentance. Job abhorred himself and repented in dust and ashes. Job forgave his friends, and God commanded that he pray for them. It follows that besides learning invaluable spiritual lessons, Job was delivered from his catastrophic predicament and rewarded for his adversities. God gave Job twice as much as he had lost of children and material riches.

(16) God is truly known only through his Son, Jesus Christ, through whom he speaks and reveals himself in these last days.

Children of God have access to God through the indwelling Holy Spirit to come near to God and speak with him. We have the blessings of intimate fellowship and communion with the Father, the Son, and the Holy Ghost.

Extraordinarily, Jesus comes into the heart of the believer and dwells there by the Spirit. Jesus is joined to believers by the Spirit. God, the Father, indwells the believer in and through the Spirit. The Holy Ghost indwells the believer whose body becomes the living temple of the Holy Ghost. An honest, in-depth examination will no doubt expose whether the believer is lacking in his knowledge of God and the intimate relationship afforded him. God works in and through believers by the Spirit to quicken, heal, and do infinitely more. We know God because he is in us and we are in him.

Scripture Reference:

Isaiah 8:13
Deuteronomy 10:12–17
Colossians 3:22
Hebrews 12:29
Romans 14:12
1 John 4:8
Psalm 62:12

Matthew 16:27
1 Peter 2:17
Deuteronomy 4:29
Numbers 12:6
Jeremiah 29:13
Hebrews 11:1–2
1 Peter 1:20

Philippians 2:1
2 Corinthians 13:14
1 Corinthians 1:9
Ephesians 2:18
1 John 1:3
the book of Job

Chapter 6

WHO ARE WE?

God created man in his own image, **in the image of God created he him**; *male and female created he them.*
— **Genesis 1:27** (emphasis mine)

And the L*ord* *God took the man, and put him into the garden of Eden to dress it and to keep it. And the* L*ord* *God commanded the man, saying, Of every tree of the garden thou mayest freely eat: But of the tree of the knowledge of good and evil,* **thou shalt not eat it: for in the day that thou eatest thereof thou shalt surely die.** *. . . And the man said, The woman whom thou gavest to be with me, she gave me of the tree, and I did eat. . . . And the* L*ord* *God said, Behold, the man is become as one of us, to know good and evil. . . . Therefore the* L*ord* *God sent him forth from the garden of Eden, to till the ground from whence he was taken.*
— **Genesis 2:15–17; 3:12, 22–23** (emphasis mine)

For as by one man's disobedience [Adam] many were made sinners, so by the obedience of one [Jesus] shall many be made righteous.
— **Romans 5:19**

But God commendeth his love toward us, in that, while we were yet sinners, Christ died for us.
— **Romans 5:8**

And it shall come to pass, that whosoever shall call on the name of the Lord shall be saved.
—**Acts 2:21**

And as it is appointed unto men once to die, but after this the judgment.
—**Hebrews 9:27**

Then shall the dust [body] return to the earth as it was: and the spirit shall return unto God who gave it.
—**Ecclesiastes 12:7**

And many of them that sleep in the dust of the earth shall awake, some to everlasting life, and some to shame and everlasting contempt.
—**Daniel 12:2**

CREATION OF MAN

(1) God created man in his own image and his likeness and blessed them. We are the offspring of God, who made man (Adam) of the dust of the ground and breathed into his nostrils the breath of life. Man became a living soul. God's breath in created man is spirit and life. God's breath in man makes man the image of God. Natural man was made an eternal, living soul after the likeness of God. It is only in God that man lives and moves and has his being. Man is God's offspring. From a rib of Adam, God made woman, Eve. The two, Adam and Eve, male and female, became one flesh created by God.

(2) Before forming man from the dust of the ground, God curiously, fearfully, and wonderfully made man in secret in the lowest parts of the earth. God also fashioned each one of us in the womb.

Adam was formed from the dust of the ground and received life from the breath of God. Eve was formed by God from Adam's rib. Subsequently, all other human beings are conceived in sin. All are born of flesh and receive natural life given by God.

Adam sinned and Adam died spiritually. All human beings are born sinners. Individuals may live spiritually and eternally only through Christ when born of the Spirit, born of God between natural birth and natural death. At such time, the believer receives the Spirit of God, of Christ, and of the Holy Spirit. God communicates, fellowships, and works with, in, and through believers by the Spirit.

(3) The first man was natural and earthy. He was the figure, symbolic of Jesus Christ that was to come. Jesus was the second man, the last Adam, who is spiritual. He is the Lord from heaven. The first Adam was made flesh and blood and is mortal and corruptible. Jesus said, "Verily, verily, I say unto you, He that heareth my word, and believeth on him that sent me, hath everlasting life, and shall not come into condemnation; but is passed from death unto life" (John 5:24). And Apostle Paul wrote to the Corinthians, "For as in Adam all die, even so in Christ shall all be made alive" (1 Cor. 15:22). The last Adam was made a quickening spirit, who was conceived by the Holy Ghost. Jesus is God with us.

(4) God's marvelous grace predestinated the called and chosen ones to be changed, to be conformed to the image of Christ. The corruptible must put on incorruption and the mortal must put on immortality. In the twinkling of an eye, at the sound of the trumpet, our vile body shall be changed that it may be fashioned like the glorious body of Jesus our Lord.

(5) From man's pre-existence to his final destination, God takes man through many stages. Man came from dust; he lives and dies. His corruptible flesh returns to dust and his spirit to God. In the intervening period, God provides the way for eternal life. By Jesus Christ, he adopts many children unto himself and gives them eternal life. God is not willing that anyone should perish.

Persons who refuse God's everlasting life are judged by God. They are appointed to everlasting punishment in the lake of fire with the beast, the false prophet, and the devil who deceived them. Those who die in their sins experience a second death. The sea, death's grip, and hell (the grave or earth) give up the dead. After this, death and hell are also cast into the lake of fire where, Jesus says, the fire is never quenched and the worm never dies.

(6) Thank God for his Son, the free gift of eternal life. Jesus is the fulfillment of God's provision of salvation for all mankind.

Scripture References:

Genesis 1:26–28, 3:19	*Genesis 2:21–23*	*Matthew 25:46*
Acts 17:27–28	*1 John 3:2*	*Revelation 20:10–15;*
Romans 5:14, 25	*Matthew 24:31*	*21:7–8*
1 Corinthians 15:45–49	*Philippians 3:21*	*2 Peter 3:9*

THE FALL OF MAN

(7) Man was made in the image and likeness of God and was given the freedom to make judgments, decisions, and choices. God granted to man specific dominion and authority in the earth. God did not void man's free will of choice after his fall into sin. Man is still free to choose to be either obedient to God's sovereign commands or to be disobedient and vainly attempt to be independent of God and self-sufficient.

THE TEMPTATION

(8) The most subtle beast of the field that God has created, the serpent, called the devil and Satan, approached Eve and enticed her and beguiled her with the first lie, because he is the father, the originator of lies. God permitted Adam and Eve to eat of the fruit of every tree of the garden except the tree of the knowledge of good and evil, which was in the midst of the garden.

God commanded and forewarned Adam that if he disobeyed him and ate of the tree of the knowledge of good and evil, he would surely die. The serpent introduced the elements of insubordination, doubt, insecurity, lust, pride, and the desire to be wise and self-assertive to Eve. Worldly instincts of lust of the flesh, lust of the eyes, and the pride of life in man were exposed.

When Adam and Eve recognized that surely they were not equal with God, they became vain in their imagination. They desired to be wise, being made subject to vanity. God took care of their vanity, however, when he subjected them to hope. This led them to have hope in God for salvation and a groaning to be clothed and whole again and to be delivered from the bondage of corruption.

GRAVE CONSEQUENCES

(9) Adam chose to doubt God's warning and sentence of death. When tempted by the serpent, first Eve ate (and then gave to Adam, who also ate) the fruit of the tree of knowledge of good and evil, explicitly prohibited by God. This simple act of disobedience appears to have been one of exploration or experimentation with the unknown. This action caused them to lose their innocence and their fellowship with God. It caused their death and separation from him. As God had warned, Adam died. Then death passed upon all men, for in Adam all die; but in Christ shall all be made alive.

EXTREME SUBTLETY

(10) First, Satan introduced doubt into the mind of Eve with the question: "Yea, hath God said, ye shall not eat of every tree of the garden?" This

was the first lie. Then Eve corrected the serpent and said: "We may eat of the fruit of the trees of the garden: but, of the fruit of the tree which is in the midst of the garden, God has said, you shall not eat of it 'lest ye die.'" Satan did not refute the truth and neither did he give up. He then inflicted the final deadly assertion. He tempted her with another distortion; that they would not surely die as God had said. The serpent, the father of lies, implied that God was not truthful to them and that God just did not want to share his power. When man ate the forbidden fruit, God said that they became "as one of us, to know good and evil." Man began to know both good and evil when Adam yielded, agreed with his wife, and also ate from the forbidden tree.

God cursed the ground with thorns and thistles, making the ground very difficult to till and to yield herbs to eat. God then drove Adam and Eve from the garden, lest they would eat of the tree of life and live forever. He placed at the east of the garden cherubims and a flaming sword to guard the tree of life.

(11) Omnipresent Jesus said that he beheld Satan, as lightening, falling from heaven. This biblical account seems to refer to Satan as the one who contrived to jeopardize man's eternal destiny. God, who created him an anointed cherub with wisdom, lived in God's holy mountain in the midst of stones of fire. Every precious stone was his covering. Iniquity, pride of beauty, and jealousy, no doubt, corrupted him. He lifted up his heart and said, I am God, and I sit in the seat of God. God judged Satan and eternally condemned him, unlike man whom God has endowed with grace and a way out of eternal damnation. God cast Satan out of the mountain of God down to the earth and diminished his power. Satan remains a terror until the time when God shall cast him into the lake of fire to be tormented forever. The battle now is on earth where Satan seeks those he might devour. God gives believers the power to overcome Satan's power.

The last enemy (death) shall be destroyed, because Jesus abolished death and brought life and immortality to light. In the end, Jesus must reign until he has made his enemies his footstool and when he shall deliver up the kingdom to God, the Father.

SEPARATIONS

(12) In his fallen state, Adam became alienated from God. He became inclined to be worldly wise, worldly minded, earthly minded, and fleshly minded. He is skeptical and unbelieving with a deceitful heart bent to wickedness and evil. After Satan understood he could not overthrow God, he demoralized man, who was made in the image of God. The fatal consequence was man's inevitable separation from his holy God. Although man was separated and driven from the presence and the close fellowship of God, our loving God had prior plans by which man could be marvelously redeemed. God would not leave Adam depraved, destitute, uncovered, and helpless.

(13) God is a God of many uncompromising separations, such as: heaven and earth, heaven and hell, day and night, life and death, eternity and time, spirit and flesh, spiritual and temporal, good and evil, righteousness and sin, incorruption and corruption, immortality and mortality.

RECONCILIATION

(14) The very first separation as revealed by the Word of God was before the foundation of the world. It was the divine separation of the Son of God from God, the Father, to come to earth at the appointed time and become the Son of Man. He was sent by the Father and came to sacrifice himself for the salvation and redemption of man and to reconcile man and all things unto himself and unto God.

Mankind was reconciled by his death and saved by his life. Jesus is the justifier who declared his righteousness for the remission of past sins committed before salvation. (Without the shedding of blood, there is no remission.)

(15) Jesus is the Advocate with the Father for forgiveness of sins committed by believers after receiving eternal salvation and upon confession

and repentance unto God. Through Jesus Christ the grace of God provides for forgiveness of any and all sin and blasphemy, except blasphemy against the Holy Ghost. And whosoever speaks against the Holy Ghost, it shall not be forgiven him, neither in this world nor in the world to come.

The subject of blasphemy arose when the Pharisees slandered Jesus, saying that he was Beelzebub and had cast out devils by Beelzebub, the prince of devils. Jesus answered them, saying, "Every kingdom divided against itself is brought to desolation; and every city or house divided against itself shall not stand" (Matthew 12:25). The Pharisees, obviously spoke falsely by implying that God acted against God, an impossibility, making it the unforgiveable sin.

Scripture References:

Psalm 139:14–16	*Genesis 2:17, 3:1–24*	*Jeremiah 17:9*
Job 10:8–9	*Romans 5:12*	*Genesis 3:21–26*
Isaiah 44:2	*1 Corinthians 15:22–26*	*John 3:16–17*
Job 31:15	*2 Timothy 1:10*	*Romans 5:10*
Isaiah 49:1, 5	*Hebrews 1:13*	*Colossians 1:20–22*
Genesis 1:26–28	*Ezekiel 28:1–19*	*Revelation 13:8*
Romans 8:20–24; 16:27	*Luke 10:17–18*	*1 John 2:1–2*
1 Corinthians 15:47–53	*John 8:44*	*Matthew 12:31–32*
2 Corinthians 5:1–5	*1 John 2:15–17*	

SALVATION FROM BEGINNING TO END

(16) After Adam's sin and God's judgment, God revealed that his plan of salvation for the redemption of man would come through the seed of the woman. God cursed the tempter serpent that beguiled the woman. He put enmity between the serpent and the woman and between the seed of the serpent and the seed of the woman, who was Jesus.

(17) Jesus was foreordained before the foundation of the world and he was manifested in these last times to die and take away the sins of man. Jesus, the Lamb of God, was slain before the foundation of the world. In the fullness of time, God sent his only begotten Son into the world to conquer sin and death, to save the world from sin, and to give eternal life to all who by faith believe in him. God, the Word, the only begotten Son of God, the Saviour, was manifested in the flesh, justified in the Spirit, seen of angels, preached unto the Gentiles, believed on in the world and received up into glory.

(18) God gives man the blessed choice to believe God and have faith in the sacrifice of his Son, Jesus Christ, for salvation and the inheritance of eternal life. Jesus Christ became man (flesh and blood) for the suffering of death to taste death for every man and to put away sin once for all. In Christ, man passes from the state of eternal death to the state of eternal life. Believers, who were sinners, are made the righteousness of God, because Jesus, who was sinless, was made sin for us.

DIVINE RESCUE WITH COVERING

(19) Adam and Eve attempted to rectify their sin of disobedience to God's command that plunged the human race into sin and death. They made themselves aprons of fig leaves in an attempt to cover their embarrassment or to mitigate the potential consequences of their deed. Adam tried to hide himself from the voice and presence of God, because he was afraid.

(20) God made coats of skin to cover them. This skin covering was a type of the substitution of the Lamb of God, who was slain before the foundation of the world to take away sin. To this day, multitudes of people try to resolve the consequence of their sin. They substitute remedies of their own reasoning and do good works believed to be acceptable to God.

(21) After God had finished conversations with Adam, Eve, and the serpent, he gave them reproof and instructions. God revealed that salvation

would come through the seed of the woman (Christ), who would bruise the head of the serpent, destroying him who had the power of death. God decreed that the serpent would bruise the heel of the seed of the woman, who would bring salvation through his humiliation, death, and resurrection. God punished Eve by sorrow in childbearing and by subjection to her husband; and Adam by having to cultivate a cursed ground, because he obeyed his wife rather than God. Eve being deceived was in the transgression.

WINNERS VERSUS LOSERS

(22) The last enemy of God that shall be destroyed is death. The righteous ones (believers) inherit everlasting life; all others everlasting punishment in the lake of fire along with death, hell, the devil, the beast, and false prophets. Believers shall be with the Lord forever.

Scripture References:

Genesis 3:1–24	*Romans 5:12–15*	*1 Timothy 3:16; 2:14*
Isaiah 7:14	*1 Corinthians 15:26*	*Hebrews 2:14–15; 9:26*
Matthew 1:18–23	*Revelation 20:10–15*	*John 5:24*
Galatians 4:4	*1 Peter 1:18–21*	*1 John 5:12*
John 8:44	*Galatians 3:16, 19*	
Genesis 2:15–28	*John 1:14; 3:16*	

AFTER EDEN—CAIN AND ABEL, VIOLENCE AND WICKEDNESS

(23) The evidence of the sin nature of man came through Cain, Adam and Eve's first child. Cain's impudence led him to bring to the Lord an offering of the fruit of the ground, which had been cursed by God. When God refused Cain's offering, Cain became incensed with Abel because

God had accepted Abel's offering of the firstling or firstborn of the flock with the fat of the animal.

(24) Abel's act of the shedding of the blood of a spotless animal was symbolic of the offering of the Lamb of God, Jesus Christ. The burning of the fat of the animal was a sweet savor unto God. This typified God's pleasure of the offering of his only begotten Son to take away sin. Jesus Christ offered himself unto God once without spot or blemish and made one sacrifice for the sin of mankind forever.

(25) Cain's violence resulted in the first shedding of human blood and the first human physical death. For this sin, God rendered the second curse of the ground, making it even more difficult to cultivate because of Abel's blood that had been shed in it.

<u>Scripture Reference:</u>
Genesis 3:17; 4:12

THE FLOOD AND NOAH

(26) When men began to multiply on the earth, the imaginations of the thoughts of man's heart were evil continually. The earth was corrupt, as man had corrupted his way, and depravity and violence greatly increased.

(27) It repented God, and it grieved him that he had made man, because of man's great wickedness. God vowed to destroy man with the earth, and he sent a great flood. Noah, a just man, walked with God. God saved him, his wife, their three sons, their wives, and male and female of every living thing of all flesh in the ark Noah built by God's command.

(28) After raining for forty days and nights, the earth was dried. Noah came out of the ark and built an altar unto the Lord. He offered burnt offerings of every clean beast and fowl. God smelled the sweet savor of the offering and said in his heart that he would neither curse the ground nor smite every living thing again as he had done with the flood.

(29) After the waters receded and the flood ended, God blessed Noah, commanding him to be fruitful, to multiply, and to replenish the earth. Of Noah's three sons, the whole earth was populated. God then allowed Noah to eat the flesh of animals. (Previously, God had permitted man to eat only green herbs for food.) Noah was forbidden to eat the flesh with the blood, which is the life of the flesh.

(30) God established his covenant with Noah that he would never again destroy the earth by flooding. God's token or sign of his covenant would be a rainbow set in the clouds, which is seen to this day, to remember his covenant with Noah.

(31) The Scriptures remind us that in the days of Noah, only eight souls were saved by water. The flood was a figure of type of baptism by water. Baptism is not a cleansing from sin. Water baptism is symbolic and reminds us of salvation through the death and resurrection of Jesus Christ. Water baptism gives believers a good conscience toward God. Jesus was baptized by John the Baptist. This act brought these endearing words from his Father: This is my beloved Son, in whom I am well pleased.

Scripture Reference:

Genesis 6:1, 5; 6:6–22; 7; 8:1–22	*Genesis 9:1–6; 9:18–19; 1:29; 9:9–17*	*1 Peter 3:20–21* *Matthew 3:17*

TOWER OF BABEL

(32) At this time in the history of mankind, all the people of the earth were one and had one language. Men became increasingly proud, self-willed, arrogant, and desired to make a name for themselves. They imagined they would be scattered abroad and decided to build a city and tower intended to reach to heaven.

REPRIMAND

(33) God was displeased with man's presumptive action and punished them by confounding their language so that they could not understand one another's speech. God also scattered them abroad over all the earth. They brought upon themselves the very thing that they had feared and attempted to avoid.

(34) They failed to make a name for themselves, except the name Babel. They built a city and a tower that could not reach unto heaven. However, God came down with retribution that stands firm to this day with respect to language barriers and dispersion abroad over all the earth.

LANGUAGE REVISITED

(35) On the day of Pentecost, God revisited the language dilemma. At that time, those present in a certain place in Jerusalem were filled with the Holy Ghost. And they began to speak in unlearned tongues, or languages, other than their own as the Spirit gave them utterance.

(36) Those who heard of this phenomenon and came from abroad thought this to be incredible. They were amazed when they heard speech in their own language, or tongue. The Holy Ghost gives the gift of tongues and interpretation of tongues unknown or unlearned, to include a total of nine spiritual gifts to believers, according to his will. The Holy Ghost, himself (not man), manifests and works these gifts in and through believers. They are: the word of wisdom, the word of knowledge, faith, the gifts of healing, the working of miracles, prophecy, discerning of spirits, diverse kinds of tongues, and the interpretation of tongues. (See 1 Cor. 12:8–10.)

Scripture Reference:

Genesis 11:1–9   Acts 2:1–18   Joel 2:28
John 15:26   1 Corinthians 14:21–22   Isaiah 28:11

ABRAHAM AND JACOB (ISRAEL)

(37) After the fall of Adam and his banishment from Eden, after Babel when God scattered the people, and before God made Israel a nation, the human race had traveled from Eden to Ur near the Persian Gulf and from Ur to Haran north of Israel. God called Abraham out of Haran and led him to Canaan to make of him a great nation, as promised.

(38) Abraham offered Isaac, his son promised by God, upon the altar as a sacrifice. God accepted Abraham's obedience, and he was spared from slaughtering his son. Isaac exemplified a shadow and type of the offering and sacrifice of Christ.

(39) God chose Isaac's son, Jacob, and changed his name to Israel. The beautiful, holy, compassionate, poetic description of God's choosing of (Jacob) Israel is matchless.

(40) The Scriptures relate: God chose a people and called them Israel. God chose her from birth when she came forth from the womb. The navel was not cut; she was not washed in water and not swaddled or clothed. No eye pitied her to have compassion upon her, but they cast her out in the open field, because she was loathed. She would have died there, but God passed by her and saw her polluted in her own blood, and said, "Live." God caused her to multiply and become great. When the time of her love came upon Israel, God spread his skirt upon her and covered her nakedness. And then God swore unto Israel, entered into a covenant with her, and said to her, "You became mine." God washed away the blood and anointed her with oil.

He clothed her lavishly, decked her with ornaments and with jewels and gold and silver, and fed her with the best of food; and she was exceedingly beautiful and prospered in a kingdom. Her beauty was perfect, for God put his comeliness upon her, and her renown was spread among the heathen. (See Eze. 16:3–14.)

(41) God proclaimed Israel to be a holy people. They were chosen to be a kingdom of priests, a peculiar treasure unto the Lord their God above all nations in praise, in name and in honor.

(42) God showed his Word to Jacob, his statutes and his judgments to Israel, but not to other nations. He dealt with her differently than he dealt with any other nation. "The LORD did not set his love upon you, nor choose you, because ye were more in number than any people; for ye were fewest of all people" (Deut. 7:7).

THE PROMISE CONSUMMATED

(43) God's providence and sovereignty in the salvation of mankind was revealed through his covenant and promise to make of Abraham a great nation and the father of many nations. Abraham believed God, and it was imputed to him for righteousness without circumcision and without the law, both of which came after the promise.

(44) Abraham was made the heir of the world through the righteousness of faith, so that it may be by grace and through faith in Jesus Christ.

Scripture Reference:

Genesis 12, 17, 21–22
Ezekiel 16:3–14
Exodus 19:5–6
Psalm 147:19–20;
105:44–45
Hebrews 8–10
Romans 9–11
Deuteronomy 14:2; 26:19
Genesis 12:1–3; 15:6, 9
Romans 4:3; 9:25; 4:13, 16

DIVISION BY REGENERATION

(45) All mankind of every nation, kindred, and tongue are sinners from natural birth. All must be born again of the Spirit of God to receive the new birth. No one shall enter into the kingdom of heaven without being born again. This is the regeneration of the natural man. It is written that flesh and blood cannot inherit the kingdom of God. Whoever believes and receives God's only begotten Son as Saviour instantly passes from a state of death into a state of everlasting life.

(46) Jesus came to earth to seek and save those who are lost. He also came to send fire and to send a sword on the earth. He came to cause division and to separate believers from unbelievers, those who inherit everlasting life from those who inherit everlasting punishment in fire and brimstone.

(47) Jesus came unto his own, the Jews, first; but they did not receive him. Then he proclaimed that anyone who would receive him, he would give them the power to become sons and daughters of God.

(48) The peoples of all the nations of the world are designated in the New Testament as belonging to one of three categories: Jews, Gentiles, or the church of God. We have previously discussed the vast distinction between the saved and the lost; the believer and the unbeliever; the righteous and the unrighteous; those who have been born once of the flesh and those who have been born the second time of the Spirit; those who have passed from death unto life and those who have not; those who are in Christ and those who are not; finally, those in all three categories either are now or shall eventually belong to one of the two divisions—saved or lost.

(49) The great salvation, translation, and regeneration bring about the eternal division. The saved are the church of God of the kingdom of God. The lost are the remaining souls who yet need the Saviour. These two categories identify all mankind. It is of the providence of God that everyone who is in Christ is a member of the church of God and of Christ.

Scripture Reference:

John 3:5–8	John 7:12, 42–43	1 Corinthians 15:22;
1 Corinthians 15:50	Matthew 24:31, 41, 46	10:32
John 5:24	John 1:10–13	Titus 3:5
Luke 19:10; 12:49–53	Romans 10:10–13	Ephesians 3:5–6
Matthew 10:34	Romans 3:23; 5:12	

THE TRANSFORMATION

(50) The church of God is composed of believers, who are the predestined, adopted, called, chosen, justified, and glorified children of God. Believers are God's inheritance and are heirs of God and joint heirs with Jesus Christ.

(51) Children of God are his elect. They are fellow citizens with all the saints of the household of God. The church, who is the body of Jesus Christ, is built upon the foundation of apostles and prophets, Jesus Christ, himself, being the chief cornerstone.

(52) In Christ, there is neither Jew nor Gentile, bond nor free, male nor female; but all are one in Christ. Jesus reconciled both Jews, who were called the Circumcision; and Gentiles, called the Uncircumcision; unto God in one body by the cross to make in himself of the two one new man.

THE PROMISE FULFILLED

(53) One of the great mysteries of God's will is that both Jews and Gentiles are partakers of God's promise in Christ by means of the Gospel. This is a glorious fellowship of the mystery, which from the beginning of the world had been hid in God. In these last days, this mystery is now manifested to his saints. Both Gentiles (once called heathens), who were far from God, separated from the commonwealth of Israel, and strangers

from the covenants and the promise; and Jews (Israelites), who were once near to God, are now one in Christ. There is now no difference, because Jesus has broken down the wall of partition that separated them, making peace between them. Jesus abolished in his flesh the enmity, the law of commandments, and ordinances, nailing them to his cross.

(54) Both Jews and Gentiles alike may be spiritually reborn by the Spirit and become completely new individuals in Christ. Before the beginning of time, God had a plan of salvation. In the fullness of time, God had a plan of salvation. In the fullness of time, God sent his only begotten Son into the world to experience the suffering of death and to taste death for every person so that he might bring many souls to glory. Jesus, the precious free gift of God to the world, became the mediator of the New Testament for all mankind.

SALVATION FORETOLD

(55) Holy men of God prophesied of this marvelous redemption. One of Isaiah's prophesies reveals God's instructions to his Son, Jesus, concerning his preplanned sacrifice for mankind. It is written that morning after morning, God instructed Jesus as to what, when, and how to speak in carrying out this great commission and sacrifice. Speaking of Jesus, the Scripture relates: "In burnt offerings and sacrifices for sin thou hast had no pleasure. Then said I, Lo, I come (in the volume of the book it is written of me,) to do thy will, O God" (Heb. 10:6–7).

(56) Jesus obeyed God, his Father. He was not rebellious, neither did he retreat in disobedience. He gave his back to the smitters and his cheeks to those who plucked off his hair. He did not hide his face from spitting. Jesus said he knew that God would help him and that, in the end, he would neither be confused nor disappointed in the predestined outcome. For the sacrifice of his life in suffering humiliation and death, God assured Jesus of

his subsequent resurrection and promised him exceedingly great rewards. It is beyond human understanding that God would allow mere mortal beings to be apprised of such knowledge and the intimacy he shared with his Son.

MESSIAH REVEALED

(57) Isaiah prophesied that God's chosen people, Israel, would not believe or receive the excellent report of the suffering Messiah.

Until the birth of Christ, God spoke to the fathers, the patriots, through the prophets. Now, in these last days, God speaks to us by his Son, Jesus Christ, the Word.

(58) During the four thousand years prior, God chose Israel and demonstrated through them acts that were only symbols, figures, signs, and shadows of the true eternal changes to come.

(59) God's marvelous works of the past leading up to the day of salvation and redemption reveal his great love, mercy, and grace.

ACTS OF GOD

(60) God provided coats of skin for Adam and Eve; the ark of salvation for Noah; God called Abraham and promised he would be the father of many nations; Jacob's name was changed to Israel; Israel becomes a nation and goes to Egypt into bondage; Moses becomes the deliverer; God exacts his last plague upon Egypt by smiting their firstborn. He spared Israel as they applied the blood of a lamb upon their door posts to memorialize their salvation from Egyptian bondage; the firstborn is smitten; God led Israel out of Egypt by way of the Red Sea; the law, commandments, ceremonies, ordinances and tabernacle are established;

God directed Moses to build a tabernacle and also an ark to house the ten commandments; Israel was humbled and tested in the wilderness and finally arrived in the promised land; God exiled Israel to Babylon for forty years for their transgression and subsequently returned them to Jerusalem; prophecy is fulfilled, for God sent Jesus into the world.

Scripture Reference:

Ephesians 1:5, 9–11	*Colossians 2:14*	*Isaiah 50:4–7; 52:13–15;*
Romans 8:28–30; 8:17	*Romans 3:20–23*	*53; 61:1–3*
2 Timothy 2:10	*2 Corinthians 5:17*	*Luke 4:18*
Ephesians 2:15–16,	*Hebrews 2:9–10*	*John 4:34*
19–22; 3:3–11	*John 3:16–17*	*Hebrews 1:1–6*
Romans 16:25–26	*2 Corinthians 9:15*	*Matthew 1*
Colossians 1:25–26	*Hebrews 9:15*	
Galatians 13:28	*2 Peter 1:21*	

MOSES, THE COVENANT, AND THE TEN COMMANDMENTS

(61) God further reveals his plan of salvation and redemption of man through Moses and the law of commandments. Adam sinned, and from this offense death reigned from Adam to Moses. It is written that the law entered that the offense might abound. The law was given by Moses, but grace and truth came by Jesus Christ.

(62) The law had its blessed purpose. The law is holy and the commandments are holy and just and good. And so are God's judgments, precepts, statutes, and testimonies. Sin by the commandment became exceedingly sinful, for by the law is the knowledge of sin.

(63) The law was added because of transgressions until the seed (Jesus) should come. The law, which came four hundred thirty years after the promise to Abraham, was our schoolmaster to bring us to Christ that we may be justified by faith.

(64) Jesus did not come into the world to destroy the law, but to fulfill the law. The law is fulfilled in love. And it is fulfilled in those who walk after the Spirit and not after the carnal flesh. The law of the Spirit of life in Christ Jesus frees us from the law of sin and death.

Scripture References:

Romans 5:14, 20
John 1:17
Romans 7:12–13
Psalm 119:137, 141, 143–145, 153

Galatians 13:17, 19, 24; 4:4
Matthew 5:17
Romans 8:1–2; 13:8–10

THE PROMISE PRECEDES LAW

(65) God's holy promise and the covenant with Abraham, which came before the law, cannot be annulled, because they are of faith. God's law of commandments is not of faith. The promise through faith does what the law could not do, because the law is weak through the flesh. The law made nothing perfect, but Jesus was the guarantor of a better testament and a better hope. By the offering of himself, Jesus has perfected forever those who are sanctified. No man is justified by the law in the sight of God. Through Christ and his grace alone, believers are justified from all things, not by the Law of Moses.

Scripture References:

Genesis 17:2, 12:2
Galatians 3:12, 17
Romans 4:13–14, 16

Galatians 2:16; 3:11
Romans 8:2–4
Hebrews 7:19–22; 10:14

Acts 13:39
Titus 3:7

NEW COVENANT ESTABLISHED

(66) Under the new covenant (the New Testament), God puts his laws into the heart of his people and writes them into their mind. Jesus took away the first covenant (the Old Testament), that he may establish the second covenant (New Testament). Jesus was made the mediator of the New Testament that by means of his death, they which are called might receive the promise of eternal life.

(67) In former dispensations, the adoption, the glory, the six major covenants, the giving of the law, the service of God, and the promises pertained to the Israelites. God's six major covenants with his servants were: two with Adam and one each with Noah, Abraham, Moses, and David. The law was a shadow of good things to come. It is written in the book that Jesus came in the flesh and was of the house and lineage of David. He took away the first covenant, as it became obsolete, that he may establish the second.

Scripture References:

Hebrews 9:15	*Psalms 147:19–20;*	*Genesis 2:15–24; 3:17–24;*
Romans 9:4–5	*105:44–45*	*6:18; 9:9–17; 12:1–3,*
Ezekiel 16:3–14	*Romans 9–11*	*7, 14–17; 17:4–12*
Deuteronomy 14:1–2;	*Hebrews 8:7–13*	*Exodus 19:3–8*
26:18–19; 32:6–21;	*Matthew 11:13*	*Deuteronomy 5:2–21*
7:6–9	*Luke 2:4*	*Hebrews 10:1–20*

PROPHESIES AND WARNINGS

(68) God chose the patriots, who were the chosen fathers, priests, prophets, and kings to speak to his people, to admonish them, to intercede for them, and to lead them in their fight against their enemies. Throughout

nearly four thousand years of history, the Israelites disobeyed their God, his laws, and his commandments.

When God chastened them—often with their enemies—they repented for a short period, but their vacillation of wickedness and repentance continued throughout many generations. God's many warnings given through his servants, from Moses to John the Baptist, were often disregarded.

(69) The prophets of past times prophesied of the sufferings of Christ, the grace, the glory, and the salvation that was to come. They also inquired and searched diligently concerning the time that Christ should come. The things they ministered then are the things which are now ministered and preached unto us by the Gospel. Even the angels desire to perceive these things, but they are not revealed unto them. The patriots of faith of former times obtained a good report, but they were not eyewitnesses of the promised advent of the Messiah. God purposed to reserve this blessed event so that they would not be made perfect without the faithful who would come after them.

Scripture References:

Deuteronomy 18:15, 18   *1 Peter 1:10–12*   *Hebrews 11:39–40*
John 5:46–47   *Isaiah 7:14–16; 9:6–7*   *Matthew 13:17*

WILDERNESS TESTINGS

(70) After spending four hundred years in Egypt in servitude, God delivered his people by his servant, Moses, and led them out of Egypt. He brought them through the wilderness on their way back to Canaan and tested them there for forty years. They were all baptized unto Moses in the cloud and in the sea. Moses was a faithful servant for a testimony (of the Gospel) to be spoken afterward. They all drank the same spiritual drink from the Rock that followed them, and that Rock was Christ.

The Israelites sinned against God and continually provoked him. They tempted God and murmured against him. They lusted after evil things and committed fornication. God tested them to see what was in their heart and whether or not they would keep his commandments. God was not pleased because of the evil deeds of his people. For this reason, he punished thousands of them very severely for their wickedness. Moses had prophesied to Israel that God would raise up among them a Prophet like unto God, whom they would hear; and that every soul that would not hear him would be destroyed from among the people.

Scripture References:

Exodus 32:6 *Deuteronomy 8:1–6* *Deuteronomy 18:15, 18–19*
Numbers 11:4; 25:1–9 *1 Corinthians 10:5–11* *Acts 3:22–23*

RETURN TO THE PROMISED LAND

(71) From the wilderness to the crossing of Jordan and back into the Promised Land, the Israelites stubbornly refused to change their evil ways. In Canaan, they ignored the prohibition to mingle with the heathen nations. They also began to worship their idols and to sacrifice to their gods.

(72) Israel's kings fought against their enemies for survival. When Israel's twelve tribes also fought among themselves, the kingdom was divided. They became Israel, the northern kingdom of ten tribes, and Judah, the southern kingdom of two tribes. There were a few good kings, but most of their kings were evil. The prophets prophesied against both Israel and Judah. God said that he, rising up early, spoke to them, but they refused to hear. God called to them, but they did not answer. The people of Jerusalem had slid back by a perpetual backsliding.

Scripture References:

1 Kings 11:29–31   Jeremiah 8:5   Isaiah 66:4

ISRAEL'S SEVENTY-YEAR CAPTIVITY AND RETURN TO CANAAN

(73) After many warnings, according to God's prophetic word, the Babylonian captivity began. It ended seventy years later when Israel and Judah returned to Jerusalem to rebuild the temple and the broken walls of Jerusalem. The first group's return was by Zerubbabel, the second by Ezra, and the third by Nehemiah.

The word of the Lord came by the latter prophets—Haggai, Zechariah, and Malachi—to admonish the people. Even after the building of Jerusalem and the temple, God said that they had profaned the holiness of the Lord, the house of the Lord, and the table of the Lord. Prophesies went forth that the Branch, the Messenger, the Lord would build the temple, the latter house, and that God would send Elijah before the day of the Lord would come.

Scripture References:

Ezra	*Haggai*	*Malachi*
Nehemiah	*Zechariah*	

Chapter 7

THE HOLY BETROTHAL AND MATRIMONY

And I will betroth thee unto me forever; yea, I will betroth thee unto me in righteousness, and in judgment, and in lovingkindness, and in mercies.

—Hosea 2:19

For I am jealous over you with godly jealousy: for I have espoused you to one husband, that I may present you as a chaste virgin to Christ.

—2 Corinthians 11:2

Wherefore, my brethren, ye also are become dead to the law by the body of Christ; that ye should be married to another, even to him who is raised from the dead, that we should bring forth fruit unto God.

—Romans 7:4

And there came unto me one of the seven angels which had the seven vials full of the seven last plagues, and talked with me, saying, Come hither, I will shew thee the bride, the Lamb's wife.

—Revelations 21:9

Let us be glad and rejoice, and give honour to him: for the marriage of the Lamb is come, and his wife hath made herself ready. . . . And he saith unto me, Write, Blessed are they which are called unto the marriage supper of the Lamb. And he saith unto me, These are the true sayings of God.

—Revelation 19: 7, 9

Transition from the Old Covenant to the New Covenant enlightens Christians significantly as to who they are. A dynamic truth is that believers are betrothed to Christ and shall be with Christ in holy matrimony at the appointed time (Hosea 2:19; 2 Cor. 11:2; Rom. 7:4; Rev. 21:9; Rev. 19: 7, 9). Christ, Bridegroom of the bride—the church—came to earth and fulfilled God's purpose. When he ascended back to heaven, he gave the church specific ministering gifts and precise instructions that are pivotal for its perfection, work, and edification (Eph. 4:8–12). This is the substance of the revelation of the mystery for the revival of the church.

As Administrator of the church, Jesus oversees the preparation of his bride. Through compliance with his provisions, the Lamb's wife also makes herself ready for the marriage supper and the wedding that will transcend all weddings (Matt. 25:1–13; Rev. 19:7–9).

JOHN THE BAPTIST

(1) Preceding the birth of Christ is the birth of John the Baptist, cousin of Jesus. Before John comes on the scene, it is noted in Scripture that God confirmed his promise to Abraham of salvation by faith, signifying the end of the Levitical priesthood and the beginning of the everlasting priesthood of Jesus Christ: "The LORD hath sworn, and will not repent, Thou art a priest for ever after the order of Melchizedek" (Psalm 110:4). And "Who is made, not after the law of a carnal commandment, but after the power of an endless life" (Heb. 7:16).

(2) John, the son of Zacharias, came in the spirit and power of Elijah to turn many of the children of Israel to the Lord their God. John was sent

from God to go before Jesus' appearing to prepare the way of the Lord. He was the voice crying out in the wilderness, as Isaiah prophesied, "Make straight the way of the Lord" (John 1:23). John preached repentance and proclaimed that the kingdom of heaven was at hand.

Scripture References:

John 1:6–28	*Luke 1:5–25; 3:2–4*	*Matthew 11:14*
Matthew 3:1–6	*Malachi 4:5–6*	

(3) The Jews sent priests and Levites from Jerusalem to John to inquire of him if he was Elias. "And he confessed and denied not; but confessed, I am not the Christ" (John 1:20). The next day John saw Jesus coming to him, and "he saith, Behold the Lamb of God, which taketh away the sin of the world" (John 1:29).

The day after that, "John stood, and two of his disciples; And looking upon Jesus as he walked, he saith, Behold the Lamb of God!" (John 1:35–36). "And the third day, there was a marriage in Cana of Galilee; and the mother of Jesus was there: And both Jesus was called, and his disciples, to the marriage" (John 2:1–2). When Jesus was told by his mother that there was no more wine for the feast, he performed his first miracle and turned water into wine. The governor of the feast said to the bridegroom that, customarily, guests are served the best wine first, but the best wine was saved until last. (See John 2:1–11.) This act of Jesus denotes that the Levitical priesthood and the law that came first are now replaced by salvation through faith and Jesus' everlasting priesthood. The best are truly last. We may also be reminded of the joy and gladness experienced by the best wine being served last and the joy and happiness Jesus, the Bridegroom, brings in coming to us in these last times.

(4) Jesus was conceived by the Holy Ghost, and born of the virgin Mary in Bethlehem, the city of David. He was born in a manger "because there was no room for him in the inn" (Luke 2:7). Jesus was born King of Israel (John 1:29).

The gospel of Matthew records Isaiah's prophesy concerning the birth of Jesus: "And she shall bring forth a son, and thou shalt call his name JESUS: for he shall save his people from their sins. Now all this was done, that it might be fulfilled which was spoken of the Lord by the prophet, saying, Behold, a virgin shall be with child, and shall bring forth a son, and they shall call his name Emmanuel, which being interpreted is, God with us" (Matt. 1:21–23).

THE BLESSED ADVENT

(5) In the fullness of time, God brought forth his Servant, the Branch. The prophesies were fulfilled. The advent of the birth of Christ Jesus the Lord came to pass.

Jesus Christ is Alpha and Omega, the first and the last, the beginning and the end. He is the only begotten Son of God; the firstborn of every creature; the Lamb of God slain before the foundation of the world; the first begotten of the dead; the firstborn from the dead.

The Word of God reveals the generation of Jesus Christ in relation to the human race: from Adam to Abraham were fourteen generations; from Abraham to King David, fourteen generations; from David to King Jechonias and the time of the Babylonian captivity, fourteen generations; and from Babylon to Christ, fourteen generations.

Scripture References:

Matthew 1–2	Luke 2	Colossians 1:15
Hebrews 1:6	Revelation 1:5; 13:8	

PRICELESS FAITH

(6) Jesus was sent into the world by God, the Father. He was conceived by the Holy Ghost in the womb of the virgin, Mary, who was chosen by God. Jesus was born in Bethlehem of Judea, the city of David.

Jesus came unto his own, but his own refused him. They did not know Jesus, nor God, nor God's ways, because they had not sought salvation by faith.

Jesus chose Israel, the Jews, first. He preached to them repentance and salvation. Israel followed after the law of righteousness, but had not attained unto it, because righteousness comes by the promise of faith that is in Christ Jesus and not by the law. While some may reject Jesus, he gives to all who receive him the power to become the sons of God, even to those who believe on his name, whether Jew or Gentile.

Scripture References:

1 Thessalonians 4:13–18	*Revelation 20:6, 14; 21:8*	*1 John 5:11–13*
Hebrews 9:27	*John 5:24*	

(7) Isaiah preached the Gospel and prophesied to Israel, but they did not believe. God included all people (both Jews and Gentiles) in unbelief that he might have mercy upon all. Salvation—the riches of the Gentiles—came through Israel's unbelief, stumbling and falling. Partial blindness also happened to Israel until the fullness of the Gentiles has been accomplished.

(8) Some of the natural branches of the good olive tree (Israel) were broken off so that branches of the wild olive tree (Gentiles), though contrary to nature, may be grafted in. God's mercy on the wild olive branches brought mercy also to Israel, so that he might have mercy on all and that Israel be grafted in again. Through the temporary casting away of the Jews, came the reconciliation of the world, and the ultimate receiving of them shall be life from the dead. Salvation is by grace through faith to all who believe. There is a remnant, according to the election of grace, and if by grace, then it is no more by the works of the law. It is written that no man shall be justified by the law in the sight of God.

(9) Jesus was foreordained before the foundation of the world, but was manifested in these last times for us. God the Word, Jesus, was manifested

in the flesh, justified in the Spirit, seen of the angels, preached to the Gentiles, believed on in the world, and was received up into glory.

Love is the fulfilling of the law. Christ is the end of the law. Love and grace reign through Christ.

Scripture References:

John 1:10–12	*Isaiah 8:14; 26:16; 52:7;*	*Galatians 2:16*
Galatians 4:4	*53:1*	*Hebrews 3; 4:3–11*
Romans 9:30–33;	*Romans 10:15–16;*	*John 8:19*
1:16–17	*11:5–32*	*1 Peter 1:20*
Matthew 1:18–25; 2:5–6	*1 Peter 2:6–7*	*1 Timothy 3:16*
Romans 3:23; 10:11–13	*John 1:11–13*	*Romans 10:4; 13:10*

PREDESTINATION, BIRTH, AND IDENTITY OF THE CHURCH

(10) God called, chose, and adopted believers to be members of the body of Christ for the praise of his glory. They are called with a holy calling, according to God's own purpose, to be holy and without blame before him in love. God adopted believers to be his children, and he predestinated them to be conformed to the image of Jesus Christ, his only begotten Son. Jesus is the firstborn among many sons and daughters of God, whom he purchased with his own blood. God also graciously and gloriously justified and glorified believers.

(11) The church, the body of Jesus Christ, consists of all those who have been saved by the blood of Jesus, born of the Spirit, and translated into the kingdom of God and of his dear Son. The church is known and designated by many names.

Some of these are: called, chosen, elect, saved, believers, children of God, sons and daughters of God, saints, servants, handmaidens, Christians, brethren, righteous, friends of Jesus, heirs of God, joint heirs with Christ, brothers and sisters of Jesus, members of the household of

God, the household of faith, the temple of God, lively stones, a spiritual house, holy priesthood, holy nation, children of light, the brethren, the temple of the Holy Ghost, the building of God, God's inheritance, and more.

<u>Scripture References:</u>

Galatians 3:26	2 Corinthians 3:3; 6:16	Hebrews 2:11
Romans 1:7; 8:14, 16–17, 21, 29	John 15:14	Ephesians 1:18
	Mark 3:35	John 1:12–13
1 Corinthians 3:9, 16; 6:19	1 Peter 2:15	1 John 3:1
	Ephesians 2:22	

DIVINE PURPOSE

(12) It is essential that the members of the body of Christ know who they are and understand God's purpose for them. The eternal Word of God and Holy Scripture provides all that is needed for Christians to know and become all that God has purposed for them. Man shall not live by bread alone, but by every word that proceeds out of the mouth of God. This word shall never pass away. It is eternal, holy, divine, immutable. Children of God have the blessed privilege to know all of the Word of God and to live by it. Christians are required to be doers of the Word and not hearers only. Those who hear and obey the Word shall be blessed in their work and deeds.

(13) The Psalms denote that God has magnified his Word above all that his hallowed name affirms (Ps. 138:2; 119:46). The Lord's word is forever settled in heaven. The redeemed of God have the Word here and will have the same Word in heaven. Christians are instructed to cease from living their lives in the flesh to the will of man and to live their lives to the will of God whose commands are mandatory.

His grace and help are provided. Believers are not their own. God purchased them with the price of his only begotten Son.

(14) God's children are to be holy as he is holy. God chastens his own, and by this means, they are made to be partakers of his holiness. God has given his children all things that pertain unto life and godliness to live godly lives. He has blessed us with all spiritual blessings in heavenly places in Christ.

(15) God's children are to be perfect as he is perfect. In Christ, we were made perfect and are also being perfected. This perfection is realized by loving, not only those who love us, but by loving our enemy and by praying for those who spitefully use us and persecute us.

The children of God are to be merciful as he is merciful. It is written in the Scriptures that both perfection and mercifulness come through the believer's acts of love.

(16) God gives his children great and precious promises that they might be partakers of his divine nature. As we behold the glory of the Lord, we are changed into the same image by the Spirit of the Lord.

(17) Christians were made righteous when Jesus, who knew no sin, was made sin for them. Believers were made free from sin to become servants of righteousness unto God. Let none be mistaken, for the Scriptures reveal that he that does what is right is righteous. Righteousness bears fruit, which leads to holiness. Without diligent adherence to this process of God's way of holiness, the believer will fail to bear the indispensable fruit of righteousness which precedes holiness. Believers who are born of the Spirit cannot sin, because the Spirit of God in them is life eternal. Transgression of the law is sin. Believers are free from the law of sin and death.

(18) When we become obedient servants of righteousness, we become servants of God, which leads to fruit unto holiness and everlasting life. The holy, eternal Word of God says that without holiness no man shall see the Lord. Holiness is a vital indicator.

(19) Christians were predestinated to be wonderfully conformed to the image of Christ. Jesus was obedient unto death and believers follow his steps, even as we are unable to fathom the depths of the humiliation, rejection, pain, and suffering he endured when he died and paid the price for the sins of every person who has lived or ever will live on earth. The children

of God are called to suffer with Christ that we may be joint heirs, that we may reign with him, and that we may be glorified together with him.

(20) Believers are taught to serve God with reverence and godly fear. Jesus feared God and so do we. The fear of God is invaluable: it is powerful and is the beginning of knowledge and wisdom; it is clean; it endures forever; it affords multiple blessings and also long life. To defy and refuse correction and instruction is to despise wisdom.

Believers are instructed to be humble and clothed with humility. God resists the proud, but gives grace to the humble. Jesus was the epitome of humility. The sinless Son of God and Son of Man agreed to leave all the glory of heaven to become sin for man to pay for the sin of man. Jesus yielded himself to die as a man at the hand of man, whom he created. God counted the soul of every human being worth saving, worth dying for, because he so loved the world.

Scripture References:

Matthew 4:4	*2 Corinthians 5:21*	*Psalm 19:9*
James 1:22–25	*Romans 6:18–23*	*Proverbs 8:13; 1:7; 15:31,*
Psalms 138:2; 119:89	*1 John 3:7*	*33; 14:26; 16:6; 22:4*
1 Corinthians 6:20	*2 Corinthians 3:18*	*Job 28:28*
1 Peter 1:15–16	*Hebrews 12:10–14*	*James 4:6, 10; 2:19*
Hebrews 12:5–14, 28	*Romans 8:17, 29*	*1 Thessalonians 5:23*
Matthew 5:43–48	*2 Timothy 2:12*	*1 John 2:17*
Luke 6:36	*Philippians 2:3–8*	*James 1:22–25*
2 Timothy 3:12	*2 Corinthians 4:8–12*	*Isaiah 50:4–9; 52:13–15;*
Ephesians 1:3	*Hebrews 12:28–29*	*53*
2 Peter 1:4	*1 Peter 2:21; 4:1*	

DIVINE GRACE

(21) God, through Jesus Christ, saved us and called us with a holy calling for his own purpose. He did not leave us to find our own way in this world of sin and iniquity, trials, and tribulations. God the Father, God the

Word, Jesus Christ, and God the Holy Ghost are in us and with us to guide us in the fulfillment of God's will. Believers are sanctified, set apart from the world, to do God's perfect will. Jesus came down from heaven not to do his will, but to do the will of his Father. It is absolutely imperative for believers to do only God's will. Jesus said he could do nothing of himself, but sought God's will. Jesus knew God's will and performed it. He finished God's work. Believers obey God, follow Jesus, and complete the work he left for us to do.

<u>Scripture References:</u>

1 Thessalonians 5:23	*James 1:22–25*	*John 4:38; 5:30; 6:38*
1 John 2:17	*Psalm 40:8*	

BELIEVERS WORK AND LABOR WITH GOD

(22) Christians work out their own salvation as God works in them according to his good pleasure.

God also has given us the great and blessed privilege of being workers and laborers together with him. We can do all things through Christ. Members of the body of Christ are ordained to continue to perform the same works as Christ during his earthly ministry, and these final works shall be even greater in number. The body of Christ has been quickened together with Christ to continue his work on earth, while also being seated together in him spiritually in heavenly places.

<u>Scripture References:</u>

Phil. 2:12–13	*Ephesians 2:5–6*	*Ephesians 1:3*
2 Corinthians 6:1	*1 Corinthians 2:10–16*	*John 8:28; 5:17–20*
1 Corinthians 3:9	*2 Peter 1:3*	*Luke 12:48*
John 15:5; 14:12		

PROVISIONS FOR THE BODY OF CHRIST

(23) Another blessing to help us in our walk and work is that we have been given the mind of Christ. God reveals things to us by his Spirit. Believers can know, understand, and discern spiritual things only by the Spirit of God, the things which the Holy Ghost teaches.

The church, the body of Christ, has been given all things that pertain unto life and godliness. We have been blessed with all spiritual blessings in heavenly places in Christ. Much has been given and much is required and expected of us. Jesus could do nothing of himself. He worked with his Father as his Father taught him. Without Jesus we can do nothing, and it is God who works in us to do his will, according to his good pleasure. All that the church is and all that she does is of Jesus and through him.

EIGHT PIECES OF ARMOR

(24) God has provided the body of Christ with effective armor necessary for protection, strength, and power to work and to stand and battle against the enemy. Armor is essential for victorious ministry and spiritual warfare against principalities, powers, rulers of the darkness of this world, and spiritual wickedness in high places. The armor enables Christians to fight and conquer the enemy spiritually, with truth, righteousness, the gospel of peace, faith, salvation, and the Word of God. The spiritual armor is compared with such protective equipment, as a shield, a sword, a helmet, and safeguards for the loins, chest, and feet.

(25) Another piece of armor is that of prayer, which is absolutely necessary for all times, for the benefit of all people, and for all ministry. Prayer is expressly commanded to be made for all saints, who are to pray always with all manner of prayer and with supplication in the Spirit. Much prayer—both individually and corporately—is vital to the life of each member and the entire body of Christ. Prayer with supplication, as well as fervent prayer, avails much more than we could ask or think.

The requirement to watch with perseverance and supplication is also a piece of armor. To pray and watch for all saints, as we are commanded, manifests love, care, and concern for the church.

Scripture References:

Ephesians 6:10–18   James 5:16   1 Timothy 2:1–4, 8

THE MYSTERY OF THE BODY

(26) As Jesus is, so is the church, who is the live, spiritual body of Christ. The church functions as Jesus, himself, administers. The church is neither a secular, political, institutional establishment nor a religious organization. The church cannot be altered. At no time can the church's functions be substituted, improvised, amended, or abridged to accommodate the will of man. The church is under the complete control of its Head and Administrator, Jesus Christ. The church is of the everlasting kingdom of God, which is not of this world. It is spiritual, within the believers, and therefore, is without outward observation. The visible kingdoms of this world shall ultimately become the kingdoms of our Lord.

(27) As Jesus is, so are we, the body of Jesus Christ. Christ was chosen before the foundation of the world and so was the church. He was crucified, died, and rose again and so did the church, the spiritual body of Christ. The church is dead unto sin, has been quickened together with Christ, is risen with him, and is alive unto God. The Spirit quickens us. The flesh gains nothing and spiritually can do nothing of itself. Since we died with Christ and rose again with him, we are spiritually alive. We are to no longer live according to fleshly lusts or to know persons or Jesus Christ according to the flesh. This is true enlightenment of the spiritual mind that brings life and peace.

(28) As Jesus was conceived of the Holy Ghost, believers are born of God of the Spirit. We, therefore, are spiritual.

We are commanded to be in the Spirit; to be after the Spirit; to be filled with the Spirit; to follow after the Spirit; to be led of the Spirit; to live in the Spirit; to love in the Spirit; to mind the things of the Spirit; to be spiritually minded; to pray in the Spirit; to preach in the Spirit; to sing in the Spirit; to speak in the Spirit; to teach in the Spirit; to walk in the Spirit; to walk after the Spirit; and to worship God in the Spirit and in truth.

(29) The church must remember and understand that God, the Father, is the Operator of all things. Jesus Christ, the Lord, the Son of God, is the Administrator of all administrations. The Holy Ghost is Manifestor, who manifests nine spiritual gifts in and through the members of the body of Christ.

The believer is to know for absolute certainty that Jesus is the Head of the body, the church, and that each believer is a member of his body. The church, the body of Jesus Christ, is one body with many members. Jesus is the Saviour of the body. Jesus loved the church and gave himself for her that he may sanctify and cleanse her. The church is the bride of Christ.

(30) The mystery of the church is unfolded to the believer who understands who the body of Christ really is and how members interact with each other and with Christ. "This is a great mystery: but I speak concerning Christ and the church" (Eph. 5:32). To know Jesus, the Head of the body, is to know the body. Unfortunately, there is a lack of knowledge as it concerns the body and its proper functions. Contrary to teachings in the Word of God, the church is highly deficient in knowledge and understanding as to its true identity and complete function.

Based on its actions, the church is in a degree of darkness, in willful ignorance, willful negligence, or disobedience as to its true spiritual correlation and composition. Being in such a state, it cannot obey and effectively perform or complete its mission and commission.

Scripture References:

Ephesians 1:22–23; 4:15;
   5:23, 30
Colossians 1:18
1 Corinthians 12:5
John 8:36; 3:3, 5
Ephesians 1:22–23
Luke 17:20–21
Hebrews 1:8; 12:28
Revelation 11:15
Ephesians 1:4
Galatians 2:20
Romans 6:3–7
Colossians 3:1–5
John 6:63

Romans 8:10–14
1 Corinthians 5:16–17
Matthew 1:20–25
John 3:5–8
1 Peter 1:23
James 1:18
1 Corinthians 15:45–50
Romans 8:8–10
Luke 9:55
1 Corinthians 2:15; 3:1;
   6:17
Romans 8:5–6, 14
Ephesians 5:1, 18
Galatians 5:16, 25

Colossians 1:8
1 Corinthians 14:14–15
Jude 20
Romans 15:19
1 Corinthians 2:4; 12:3;
   14:2, 4–5, 13; 2:4; 18:25
Romans 12:7
John 4:23–24
1 Corinthians 12:4–6,
   12–28
Romans 12:4–9
Ephesians 4:4–16;
   5:23–33; 5:25–32
1 Corinthians 12:18–28

BODY FUNCTIONS

(31) Who is the body of Christ? How does this spiritual body function? The Word of God enlightens us by comparing the spiritual body with the natural body. First of all, Jesus is the one and only Head of the spiritual body, consisting of many members (parts). These spiritual parts of the body are compared with the natural body parts, such as the foot, hand, ear, eye, and nose. Each natural body part has its particular function. Each part is joined together and depends on, cares for, and works together in conjunction with the other. The same is true of each individual believer, which makes up the whole spiritual body of Christ.

JESUS GIVES MINISTERING GIFTS

(32) Each member of the body of Christ is to know and understand that as a vital functioning part of the body, he has received a ministering

gift. When Jesus ascended to the Father on high, he led captivity captive. When he rescued his own, he gave five ministering gifts to the body of Christ. He gave some apostles, some prophets, some evangelists, some pastors, and some teachers.

Through these five ministering gifts, three vital objectives and purposes of the church would be realized. First, all members of the body of Christ would be perfected to equal its holy calling and purpose. Second, the work of the ministry begun by Jesus in his earthly ministry of salvation, healings, and deliverances would continue and be multiplied. Third, the entire body of Christ would be edified in love as each believer (member part/ministering gift) recognizes and acknowledges its Head and also its body. Every believer has at least one ministering gift given to them by Jesus. The body works together as a whole in obedience to its Head and Administrator, Jesus, as he directs and administers.

GOD ASSIGNS MINISTERING GIFTS

(33) God has set every member in the body of Christ and has placed them within the body as it pleased him. God, himself, has tempered the body together, giving more abundant honor to the part that lacked equal ability so that no part (believer) would be inferior or function inadequately. In great contrast, man's buildings of plaster, brick, and untempered mortar are lifeless.

The order in which God has set each member in the body is: first, apostles; second, prophets; third, teachers; after that miracles, gifts of healings, helps, governments, and diversities of tongues. These ministries and functions are of importance and value relative only to body function, not of hierarchy, superiority, or inferiority of person or office.

Every believer who has been saved by the blood of Jesus, born of the Spirit, and translated into his kingdom is a member of every other believer. Each and every believer must actively function, or, if not, will degenerate and become useless.

(34) Believers must be aware that of utmost importance is God's divine desire, design, plan, purpose, will, Word, and work for the church before the foundation of the world. It shall come to pass that Jesus, our Saviour, shall sanctify and cleanse the church by the Word that he may present it to himself a glorious church. At that time, the church shall be holy, without blemish, unblamable, and unreprovable in his sight.

GIFTS AND WORK OF THE HOLY GHOST

(35) Members of the body of Christ are given the gift of the Holy Ghost, who was promised by God, the Father. It is written that the Holy Ghost could not come to the earth until Jesus had been resurrected, had ascended to the Father, and the day of Pentecost had fully come.

Jesus, our Lord, our Head, and our leader, was baptized in the water. Immediately afterward, the Spirit of God descended upon him. Jesus was filled with the Holy Ghost and was led by the Spirit into the wilderness to be tempted by the devil. After forty days, the devil left him and the angels ministered unto him. Then Jesus began to teach in the synagogue to fulfill Scripture.

The obedient church, the body of Christ, follows Christ Jesus, their example, in baptisms, in temptations, in sufferings, in the baptism of death, in resurrection, and in ministry.

(36) The Holy Ghost, who was given by God to the church, nevertheless, is so unfamiliar to so many believers. Before salvation, believers were reproved by the Holy Spirit: of sin, of righteousness, and of judgment. As Jesus was conceived of the Holy Spirit, believers were born of the Spirit. The Holy Spirit indwells believers. He baptizes all believers into one body, the body of Jesus Christ.

(37) God, the Holy Ghost, the Holy Spirit, the Spirit of God, Spirit of Christ, the Comforter is also identified as the Spirit of Grace, the Spirit of Life, and the Spirit of Truth.

The Holy Ghost is the believer's guide, helper, intercessor, leader, reminder, revelator, and teacher.

(38) Jesus baptizes obedient, yielded believers with the Holy Ghost, who bestows, reveals, and works the gifts. These gifts are: the word of wisdom, word of knowledge, faith, gifts of healing, working of miracles, prophecy, discerning of spirits, tongues, and the interpretation of tongues.

(39) The Holy Ghost is the Manifestor. He manifests and works these nine spiritual gifts in and through members of the body of Christ so that the church as a whole may prosper.

The church suffers great spiritual deficiencies when these gifts are either unknown, neglected, or lie dormant within believers. These spiritual gifts are extremely valuable, because they assist the members as they minister according to the ministering gifts given to the church by Jesus Christ.

BODILY ACTIVITY OR INACTIVITY

(40) Who is the church and what activities are required of it? The church is the spiritual body of Christ. It can be compared with the natural body of man as to function and activity. The whole body functions together as uniquely designed. As each body part becomes aware of its existence then comes exercise, growth, and maturity in conjunction with the entire body as directed by its Head, Jesus Christ. Unfortunately, to its detriment, the body is deficient and under-productive, because the vast majority of the members of the body of Christ do not know which member they are. They have not been taught and, therefore, do not understand that they are designated a particular vitally functioning, ministering part of the body.

(41) The body of Christ functions as a whole. The natural body, consisting of parts, as hands, feet, eyes, ears, nose, mouth, and other parts is one body. The church, likewise, is one complete working body of: apostles, prophets, evangelists, pastors, teachers, and also helps and governments. All members (parts) work together as one.

THE HEAD OF THE BODY

(42) The one Head is Christ. Comparatively, in the natural body, the hand cannot be the foot, neither the eye the ear. Can the hand walk or the eye smell or the ear speak? Can any other part be the Head?

THE SUPREME OPERATOR

(43) God is the Operator of all things, of heaven, of earth, and of the church. God sets the members (parts) of the body of Christ in the church to conform to his purposes and to please himself. He placed the apostles first, the prophets second, and the teachers third. After these, he placed miracles; then gifts of healings; helps (i.e., singers, musicians); governments (i.e., deacons, various administrations); diversities of tongues. Every believer is vital, is different one from the other in function, but each complements and depends on the other. God tempered the body together and operates all parts (ministries) together in conjunction with each other.

ADMINISTRATOR OF THE CHURCH

(44) Jesus is the one and only Administrator and the Head of the church, his body. Jesus is the only leader, who is in charge and in control of the church. No other being can be in charge or in control or is the head or leader of the church.

When Jesus ascended up on high, he led captivity captive and gave gifts (ministering gifts) unto men. He gave some apostles, some prophets, some evangelists, some pastors, and some teachers. As Administrator, Jesus administers, directs, executes, governs, guides, conducts, leads, etc., concerning all of the members of his body.

THE FOUNDATION CORNERSTONE

(45) Jesus is the chief cornerstone and the foundation of his body, the church, which was laid before the world began. The apostles and prophets are essential members of the body relative to function, because they are a part of the foundation with Jesus. The preordained foundation has been put in place, built upon, supported, and sustained by its Head. From its Head, every believer of the whole body is succinctly joined together. All parts are measured, and they equally and effectively support one another so that the whole body may increase and edify itself in love.

By God, the Father, the Operator; through the Word, Jesus Christ; and with the Holy Ghost, the Holy Spirit; the mystery of the church, the body of Jesus Christ, is unveiled beginning with its foundation.

Scripture References:

John 3:3–8
Romans 8:8–11
1 Corinthians 12:12–28
Ephesians 5:26–27
Colossians 1:22

Ephesians 4:8–16
2 Timothy 1:9
Ezekiel 13:10
1 Thessalonians 4:16
Revelation 21:2

2 Peter 3:10
Romans 12:4–8
1 Corinthians 6:15

APOSTLES

(46) The ministering gift of apostle was given by Jesus, and God set the apostle first within the body of Christ.

It is written that apostles are called by Jesus Christ by the will of God and not of men or by man. A true apostle knows that he has met all of the unique prerequisites and criteria of his calling. He knows that he is part of the foundation with Jesus and with the prophets.

(47) Apostles are sent forth. They go to local churches and remain as long as necessary. Apostles receive revelations from the Lord. They perform

signs, wonders, and mighty acts. They suffer infirmities, reproaches, necessities, persecutions, and distresses. By revelation, God made known to the apostles and prophets the mystery of Christ and of the church.

(48) Apostles declare the entire counsel of God. They preach the gospel, teach, heal the sick, raise the dead, cast out devils, cleanse the lepers, lay hands on for baptism of the Holy Ghost, and more. Apostles, with Jesus, take care of the church. Apostles have an indispensable ministry. They know the church's true composition. They are fully aware of its state (condition), its correct as well as its incorrect doctrines. As part of the foundation on which the church is built and on which it stands, they receive knowledge and instruction firsthand from Jesus.

(49) The Apostle Paul's experiences are extraordinary and typical of apostles. He wrote: "It is not expedient for me doubtless to glory. I will come to visions and revelations of the Lord. I knew a man in Christ above fourteen years ago, (whether in the body, I cannot tell; or whether out of the body, I cannot tell: God knoweth;) such an one caught up to the third heaven.... How that he was caught up into paradise, and heard unspeakable words, which it is not lawful for a man to utter" (2 Corinthians 12:1–2, 4). Counter to this miraculous blessing, Paul suffered infirmities, yet he glorified God in them.

(50) Apostles maintain the church. They correct doctrines and teachings, eradicate heresies, and reprimand immorality. The true body of Christ and its foundation never changes. Mere mortals are originators and promoters (knowingly or unknowingly) of unscriptural denominational divisions and doctrines that divide and cause contention. Multitudes of untenable errors have rendered the church great spiritual retrogression, degeneration, and decline. Conclusively and inconclusively, the deterioration and critical condition of the church is directly attributable to the conspicuous absence of the apostles, as well as inattention to the only foundation which Jesus, himself, has laid.

PROPHETS

(51) Prophets are the chosen part of the foundation who receive messages from Jesus and from God for the church. God set the prophets second within the body of Christ. They foretell, forewarn, exhort, admonish, as well as edify and comfort the church.

(52) Major prophets of God, as Isaiah, Jeremiah, Ezekiel, Daniel, and John the Baptist proclaimed God's timely, urgent, compelling, and imperative messages. Today's prophets of the church have comparable assignments. Prophets are sent by God and have little honor where they are known. They speak disciplinary and punitive words and also perform powerful miracles. By revelation of God, apostles and prophets were given the mystery of Christ and of the church.

EVANGELISTS

(53) Evangelists are given this ministering gift by Jesus. They have a deep compassion for lost souls. Their primary responsibility is to preach the gospel.

They go into all the world and preach the gospel to every nation. They do so without fear or concern for the cost. Souls are saved and added to the church.

(54) To the world's deprivation and the church's void, no doubt, multitudes of evangelists remain dormant and unprepared. Some are in church attendance, but they are inactive, due to lack of training and discernment of their calling as an evangelist. Many who are aware of this important ministering gift may be frustrated, not knowing that they form part of the entire body that works together to bring saved souls into the congregation of the believers for nurture and growth.

PASTORS

(55) For generations, indisputably, the pastor has been the most visible member of the body of Christ in local churches. The pastor, under-shepherd to the Chief Shepherd, is overseer of his flock. He is responsible to watch over them, to discern their needs, and to take care of them. He is an example for the flock and not a lord over them. (There is only one Lord of all and over all.) He ministers willingly and with a ready mind as directed by Jesus Christ and God, the Father.

(56) Pastors receive apostles and prophets sent by Jesus to their church. Apostles know the biblically correct embodiment, doctrines, teachings, and practices of the church. As part of the church's foundation, apostles and prophets know truth from error as well as gross deficiencies of the church.

Prophets warn and admonish those who, biblically, are far off course and embrace error, knowingly or unknowingly. Pastors may receive only from God fresh manna for believers in his care.

(57) It is the pastor's duty and responsibility to permit apostles to correct erroneous doctrines, teachings, and practices of the church. These include: its structure, baptisms, baptism of the Holy Ghost, ministering gifts, spiritual gifts, tithing, the law, morality, and much more, upon which the church is built and sustained.

(58) Elders, who are called to be pastors, have the same exact duties as pastors and bishops, working together. Pastors are responsible to see that every member does his part. As part of the whole body, the duties of the pastor, naturally and comparatively speaking, can be compared to a maestro who conducts the entire orchestra; a school principal who directs all facets of school activities; a manager or coach, and so on. The distinct difference is spiritual and all three interact and act together with the body of Christ, consisting of apostles, prophets, evangelists, pastors, teachers, and also helps and governments.

(59) There are no scriptural entities, divisions, separations, enumerations, or nomenclatures of clergy and laymen. Repetitive, perpetual errors are to be corrected, revoked, and replaced with truth. Pastors reject filthy lucre. They are gifted with discernment and wisdom. The shepherd discerns the enemies and protects the Chief Shepherd's flock from wolves.

(60) Divisions must be abandoned and eradicated and the one church shall emerge victorious. This should occur as God sends apostles and prophets to churches to do their work. And when pastors and congregations receive their counsel, reproof, and instruction, believers shall be revived, refreshed, restored, and confirmed in the Word of God. (See Eph. 2:20–22; 2 Cor. 11:28; Acts 11:27; Acts 15:32.) Neither pastor, evangelist, teacher, nor any other member of the body of Christ has been chosen or ordained to function in this capacity. Paul, however, was also called to be a teacher and preacher. Apostle Paul wrote to the Galatians (chapter 1, verse 1): "Paul, an apostle, (not of men, neither by man, but by Jesus Christ, and God the Father, who raised him from the dead.)"

When believers, the true building of God, who assemble in buildings (some of brick and mortar), are truly receptive and receive God's messengers, they shall be truly revived and built up inwardly to the glory of God. Unlike the itinerant apostle and evangelist, the pastor is responsible to see that every believer in his care knows his calling, ministering gift(s), and spiritual gifts. All pastors, bishops, and elders of their local church develop and prepare every believer in their assembly to function together as the body of Christ. Adherence to the truth will bring regenerative power and will end perpetual error, inertia, and atrophy in the church.

TEACHERS

(61) Jesus gave to the body the ministering gift of teacher. God chose to set the teacher third in order in the body of Christ after the apostles and

prophets. This shows the value God has given to the teaching function and ministry. The teacher receives from God, Jesus, and the Holy Spirit profound truths and revelatory knowledge of the Word, not according to natural ability or professional expertise. They are anointed to instruct the church how to be taught of God, of Jesus, and of the Holy Spirit, who are the true teachers.

(62) Ordained chosen teachers teach the whole counsel of God—from the rudimentary "milk" to the advanced "strong meat." As believers mature, they learn to discern many things, including which ministering and spiritual gifts have been given them. They become active workers for God and with God rather than remaining idle spectators in the congregation.

(63) Teachers are indispensable to church growth. Absence or neglect of the use of this vital ministry gift in the church is extremely serious. As a result, God's people are destroyed and the church is devastated for lack of knowledge. The Word of God is being greatly compromised, both as taught and supposedly lived. Believers are deceived by false teachers, whom they willingly choose to hear, rather than readily choose sound doctrine and truth. This obstinacy has led to spiritual deafness, famine, and emaciation, not because of unavailability of the Word, but because of the inability to hear the Word of God due to the rejection of truth.

(64) In obedience to God and his Word, pastors must recognize teachers among the congregation and allow them to exercise their ministering gift together with all other ministries and gifts. Then spiritual famine shall cease, knowledge of the truth shall abound, and the church shall flourish.

Scripture References:

1 Corinthians 9:1	*2 Corinthians 11:28; 12:7, 12*	*Matthew 23:34; 11:11; 22:9*
Galatians 1:1		
2 Corinthians 1:1	*Ephesians 3:1–7; 4:11*	*Luke 14:23*
Ephesians 1:1	*1 Corinthians 12:28*	*Hosea 4:6*
Colossians 1:1	*Acts 20:27*	*Amos 8:11*
Matthew 10:16	*Ephesians 2:20–22*	*1 Samuel 15:18–23*
Romans 15:19	*Mark 6:4*	

DIVINE PROVISION: COMFORTER AND HELPER

(65) Upon his return to the Father, as promised the disciples, God sent the Comforter, the Holy Ghost, into the world to take the place of Jesus' visible presence. As mentioned previously, the Holy Ghost indwells believers, baptizes them into one body, gives them nine spiritual gifts, and manifests these gifts in and through the members to help them to be an effective church. These nine spiritual gifts are activated and become known when the believer is baptized by Jesus with the Holy Ghost. These gifts are vital for believers who are yet in mortal flesh. As it is written, prophesies shall fail, tongues shall cease, and knowledge shall vanish. We shall know perfectly when immortality and incorruption shall supersede mortality and corruption. For now, these gifts are invaluable.

(66) Believers need to know the person of the Holy Ghost. Just as sure as salvation is received by faith; just as the sinner believes the gospel and earnestly desires, seeks, and asks for forgiveness of sins, and receives eternal life; the same is true of the promise of the baptism of the Holy Ghost. When the believer by faith earnestly desires, seeks, and asks Jesus to baptize him with the Holy Ghost, he shall receive him, after which the spiritual gifts shall be manifested in and through him by the power of the Holy Ghost within.

(67) The promised Holy Ghost manifested himself on the day of Pentecost to the disciples and company in Jerusalem in the upper room. People of many nations heard of this and they gathered there. They were confounded by this miraculous event and some mocked. Beginning with the Old Testament prophecy of Joel, Peter explained this great advent to inhabitants of Judah and Jerusalem. When the Jews heard this, they were disquieted in their spirit and asked what they should do. Peter replied that they should repent and believe in Jesus that they may receive the gift of the Holy Ghost.

(68) The Tower of Babel was the time and place of God's judgment when he divided and dispersed the people, originating separate nations with diverse languages. Pentecost was the event heralding a reversal of the former dilemma. As the Holy Ghost filled them and gave them utterance,

the believers began to speak unlearned languages of the many nations gathered there.

(69) This phenomenon was God's way of revealing to mankind that he was uniting, as one, all peoples of all nations and languages. That one union is in, by, and through One, the Lord Jesus Christ, and is manifested by the Holy Ghost.

Scripture References:

Luke 24:49	Mark 1:8	John 1:33
Matthew 3:11	Luke 3:16	Acts 1:4–8; 2:1–18

CALL FOR REPENTANCE

(70) Believers must be aware of the critical condition of the church and their accountability to God for obedience. The church's first response should be to begin with unceasing prayer and repentance for all sins and errors, both individually and collectively. This is the only starting point. It is time for the church to seek the face of God and agree with him and his Word. Believers surely must realize that the current degeneracy is absolutely untenable. Such dire predicament of the church reveals that transformation is far overdue and urgent.

(71) Prayer and repentance that conform to the Scriptures will avail much. This is prerequisite to forgiveness, correction, renewal, and restoration by Almighty God. Faith and thanksgiving are also vital components of prayer. As taught in the Word of God, prayer is to be abundant, constant, and fervent. It requires sacrifice.

(72) Prayer, confession, and repentance expose the most grievous errors and serious omissions that have plagued the church for generations and centuries. Without acknowledgment, correction and renewal, it will be impossible for the church to be forgiven and restored. It is written that the church shall prevail; however, believers must choose whether to go the way

of God or not. The act of repentance brings about godly fear and godly sorrow that result in reversals of decades of spiritual decline. This requires adherence to the Word of God to abolish and abandon every word and deed that conflict with the eternal, holy Word of God. And this word is profitable for doctrine, reproof, correction, and instruction in righteousness.

(73) The church is to be to the praise and glory of God, who is supremely worthy. Granted, a son honors his father, and a servant honors his master. If God is our heavenly Father, then where is his honor? If God is our Lord and Master, then where is his fear? If we disobey and sin willfully, judgment awaits us.

(74) The time has come that judgment must begin at the house of God. Every one of us shall give account of himself to God. We must all appear before the judgment seat of Christ. The fear of the Lord is wisdom and to depart from evil is understanding. To hear and obey is better than any sacrifice of our choosing.

(75) The Word declares that at a certain season, there were some who told Jesus that Pilate had mingled the blood of some Galileans with their own sacrifices. Jesus' reply was that they supposed these Galileans suffered such things because they were sinners above all Galileans, and if they did not repent, they would all perish likewise.

(76) Besides abstaining from willful sin, perpetual confession, repentance, and cleansing are necessary throughout our lifetime. God's requirements of confession and repentance involve putting away bitterness, wrath, anger, blasphemy, clamor, evil speaking, malice, filthy communication, and also forgiving others even as God forgives us. When believers attempt to dishonor God's commands, we pray, ask, and do not receive because of wars, fightings, killings, and lustings. These evils come when believers are friends of the world, have enmity against God, and are enemies of God. When children of God envy the world and lust after evil things, the Spirit that dwells within them grieves enviously, due to their apathy, ambivalence, or carnal choice. We are to sanctify the Lord God in our hearts, let him be our dread and our fear, obey his voice, and cleave unto him.

(77) Believers who are spiritually sleeping appear also to lack the ability to grasp the significance and the meaning of what they see naturally. There seems to be little or no concern or alarm in the face of things such as: phenomenal calamities, plagues, dreaded diseases, tormenting mites, debasing pornography, demonic activity, as well as tragic escalating atmospheric turbulence. Iniquity abounds and the love of many has grown cold. Jesus questioned whether he would find faith in the earth when he comes again. It is time to pay strict attention to Jesus' warnings of recurring sorrows, wars, rumors of wars, distress of nations, famine, and earthquakes.

(78) Jesus prophesied that as it was in the days of Noah, so shall it be when he is revealed at his coming. The people ate, drank, married, and were given in marriage until the day that Noah entered into the ark and the flood came and destroyed them all. The warning, intrinsically, concerned not so much as what they were doing, but what they were failing to do. They ignored warnings and disobeyed the Word of God. Jesus also admonished that as it was in the days of Lot, the people ate and drank, bought and sold, planted and built, but in the same day that Lot went out of Sodom, it rained fire and brimstone from heaven and destroyed them all. These activities persist today. They are pursued and doubtless shall exist when Jesus comes. The red flags are voluminous. Again, the people perished for refusing to heed God's warnings.

(79) The coming of the Lord draws near. When Jesus comes again and the kingdom of God appears, the wise and obedient bride of Christ shall be ready to meet him. In another parable, there were those who slept and neglected to watch and be warned.

When they finally awoke, it was too late, and they were refused entry into the kingdom. It would be wise for the church to heed the Word of God to watch, pray, and be ready. Procrastination indicates unbelief and tends toward backslidings. The parable cautions us that it is difficult, if not impossible, to catch up, especially in view of ample forewarnings, examples, and instructions. When we do not fear God and abhor sin, we try to convince ourselves that God will not take it into account.

REPENTANCE EQUATES REVERSAL

(80) The Word of God reveals that it will be impossible for those who fall away to be renewed again unto repentance. For those who sin willfully, having received the knowledge of the truth, there remains no more sacrifice for sin for them, as they crucify to themselves the Son of God afresh.

God's work in time past to his people says that when he would punish the land with famine and desolation because of their transgressions, even if faithful men, such as Noah, Daniel, and Job were in it, these men would deliver only their own souls by their own righteousness. Jesus says that every one of us shall give account of himself to God.

The church of today must realize that it is in the valley of decision, wandering in the wilderness. It is asleep and it is time to awake out of sleep and arise from the dead and Christ will give us light.

The way of God requires no less than that the church immediately repent and make a 180-degree turn from sin, error, and disobedience to righteousness, obedience, and holiness.

GOD'S HOUSE OF PRAYER

(81) The local church of God and of Jesus Christ is the house of prayer. The church is to seek, desire, and strive earnestly, diligently, and urgently and see to it that it becomes a house of prayer for all people. The apparent inadequacy of prayer has led to enormous deficiencies, depleting the very life of the church, individually and collectively. Only a profusion of prayer with repentance in the church will bring about God's unprecedented revival.

(82) Prayer should be accepted and regarded as pre-eminent in the church. It is incomprehensible how prayer, instead of being a primary function in the church, is practically last in importance. The entire church gathering must faithfully engage in regular, consistent prayer for many hours. It is essential that the church be taught the absolute necessity of

prayer, how to pray, what to pray, and when. A common weakness among believers is to neglect prayer. Christians are to pray much, both individually and privately. Prayer is like a lifeline to God and is extraordinarily beneficial for us. Prayer is a precursor to miracles, answers and solutions, power, spiritual maturity, knowledge of, and intimacy with God.

(83) To pray with the spirit and with understanding is effectual prayer. To pray always and without ceasing requires wisdom and may at first call for great diligence and persistence. To pray according to the holy will and Word of God is unparallel to any other practice of prayer. Praying in this manner increases one's faith to expect and receive answers to requests and petitions. (See 1 John 5:14–15.) Fasting with prayer yields miracles.

(84) Jesus prayed to his Father, who heard and answered his Son. We are exhorted to live by the faith of the Son of God. We pray in the name of Jesus, our mediator and intercessor, because he sacrificed his life for us and reconciled us to God. Believers can pray with confidence, knowing that God hears us and that we have the petitions that we desire of him. We have confidence in God, because we keep his commandments and do the things that please him.

(85) Prayer is truly a dynamic endowment from God. Prayer of confession is necessary for forgiveness. Prayer with praise is exhilarating. Prayer of thanksgiving is satisfying, as God is praised for his excellent greatness and mighty acts to the children of men.

(86) The church assembly, first of all, is exhorted that supplications, prayers, intercessions, and thanksgiving be made for all mankind everywhere who are in need of salvation. This, obviously, covers every lost soul on the face of the earth. God is omnipresent.

Our prayers go to the places where God is and where we are not and cannot be. Those whom God calls and sends go prayerfully and in power and preach the gospel. Obedient Christians assist when they pray for these evangelists and for the lost souls. God answers, Jesus saves.

(87) Second of all, the church assembly is instructed to pray for all saints (all of the body of Christ throughout the world) always, with all

prayer and supplication in the spirit, watching with all perseverance and supplication. (Refer to other sections on prayer.)

Scripture References:

1 Timothy 2:8	*1 Peter 4:17*	*Romans 14:11–12;*
Ephesians 6:18	*Hebrews 6:4–8; 12:14*	*3:11–18*
Luke 18:1	*Ezekiel 14:14*	*Job 28:28*
Matthew 3:8	*2 Timothy 2:19*	*1 Samuel 15:22–23*
Mark 11:22–26	*Isaiah 56:7*	*Deuteronomy 13:4*
1 Corinthians 14:15	*Matthew 21:13, 22*	*Isaiah 8:13*
1 Thessalonians 5:17	*Luke 19:45–46*	*Matthew 24*
2 Corinthians 7:10	*2 Chronicles 7:1–2, 14–15*	*Luke 18:8; 17:26–30*
Proverbs 1:20–33	*Ephesians 4:21–32*	*James 5:7–8*
Luke 13:1–9	*James 4:1–17*	*Luke 21:28*
Hebrews 4:12–13;	*Colossians 3:8–16; 4:2*	*James 4:8*
10:26–31	*Mark 1:35*	*Romans 13:1*
Malachi 1:6	*Jude 1:20–21*	*2 Thessalonians 2:2*
James 5:13–20	*1 John 3:21–22; 5:14–15*	*Philippians 4:5*
1 John 1:8–10	*2 Corinthians 5:10*	*1 Peter 4:7*

INDIVIDUAL (PRIVATE) PRAYER

(88) Believers, no doubt, are inclined to be diligent in the practice of individual, private prayer. Those who take ample time to pray, both individually and corporately, will be blessed exceedingly beyond measure. As we come before God's throne of grace, the Word of God gives us details on cleansing. Recorded in the book of Leviticus, this is worthwhile to consider for our learning, as we are cleansed when we confess our sins. The priests, Levites, and high priest were required to cleanse themselves, their garments, vessels, the altar, surrounding areas, and more. There was washing with water, sprinkling of blood, consecration, purification, and anointing with oil before entering into the holy place, before the mercy seat, and before God to make atonement for sins.

Jesus warned that it would be better to pluck out the eye or cut off hand or foot and enter into life maimed than to go into hell. Likewise it would be better to pierce through one's heart with a spear to be severed from the tenacious bondage of lust. God forgives sin, Jesus' blood cleanses from all sin, and believers are cleansed by the Word.

(89) The Lord's Prayer shows the requirement of at least daily prayer and confession. (All mankind can relate to the necessity of perpetual fleshly body cleansing, due to continual defilement.) Believers are taught by Jesus to pray in secret to include personal prayer and confession of sins. We are taught not to be reluctant to abase ourself, for if we abase ourself, we shall be exalted. Our vile body, eventually, shall be fashioned like unto Jesus' glorious body.

(90) The following personal prayers are no secret, but are from the Word of God and may be prayed privately:

> Father, in the name of Jesus, I pray that you would please forgive me for every sin, iniquity, transgression, abomination, vileness, uncleanness, filthiness, wrong doing, and wickedness that I have committed against you in thought, word, and deed. I have sinned and come short of your glory.
>
> Father, in the name of Jesus, please forgive me for every sin, iniquity, trespass, abomination, vileness, uncleanness, filthiness, wrong doing, and wickedness that I have committed against my neighbor in thought, word, or deed. I have hated my neighbor instead of loving my neighbor. I have judged my neighbor instead of not judging my neighbor.
>
> Cleanse me from secret faults and keep me back from presumptuous sins. Father, I cleanse myself of filthiness of the flesh and of the spirit, perfecting holiness in the fear of God.

(91) We are to confess our faults one to another and to speak no evil, but love one another. Can both bitter and sweet water originate from the same spring? Can we curse men while we also bless God? In assuming such, there is neither logic of man nor wisdom that comes from above. We pray and give thanks and do all to the glory of God in the spirit. Nothing is left to the flesh except yielding, obedience, sacrifice, and dedication.

As we have prayed, we are to be certain that we have forgiven every one who has sinned and trespassed against us and also that we have asked the same forgiveness of whomever we have sinned and trespassed against, in person whenever possible. This being done, we can know that we have a good conscience toward God, and that God has answered us.

(92) We should always show gratitude:

> Father, I thank you for forgiving me and cleansing me from all unrighteousness. I thank you and praise you for your excellent greatness, for your mighty acts, and for your wonderful works to the children of men. I admire you and adore you. I exalt you and extol you and praise your holy name.

(See also the section on Praise, Worship, and Thanksgiving.)

(93) Personal prayer, no doubt, would not be complete without interceding and praying for these: beginning with the closest of kin to the most distant extended family and in-laws; then past, present, and future friends and acquaintances; neighbors, business associates, and associations; ex-playmates, schoolmates, educators, employers, and co-workers. Among these may be those whom we have had opportunity to witness to, but for some reason neglected to do so. Our prayers, whether privately or corporately, covering all people identified as individuals, categories, and groups, will necessarily contain duplication, which is perfectly fine.

(94) Prayer and meditation shows God that we will not allow activities and cares of this world to rob us of the coveted intimacy, fellowship, and

communion with him. Prayer affords us access to God's revelations, visions, dreams, and instructions as to his will for our lives.

(95) Psalm 103 summarizes the most magnificent inclusive expression of gratitude, of praise, and of thanksgiving to God that one could imagine. As the psalmist, we may bless the Lord in our soul and all that is within us, which are our spirit and the quickening Spirit of God. The flesh profits us nothing. We should not cease to bless the Lord for all of his incomparable benefits: God forgives all our iniquities; heals all our diseases; redeems our life from destruction; crowns us with loving kindness and tender mercies; satisfies our mouth with good things so that our youth is renewed like the eagle's.

God has not dealt with us according to our sins nor rewarded us according to our iniquities. As the heaven is high above the earth, so great is his mercy toward those that fear him. As far as the east is from the west, so far has he removed our transgressions from us. As a father pities his children, so does the Lord pity those who fear him, because God knows our frame and remembers that we are dust. God is infinitely gracious. We are definitely unworthy.

Our heavenly Father desires intimacy with his children. He cherishes this loving companionship made possible because we are in Jesus. "No man hath seen God at any time; the only begotten Son, which is in the bosom of the Father, he hath declared him" (John 1:18). In the garden of Eden, Adam felt the presence of God. It follows that this private encounter with God was interrupted and subsequently lost because of sin. Through Christ we have the blessed privilege of personal communication with God, our Father. We look forward to having conversation with our loved ones and friends. Would we be less eager and not elated to have frequent conversation and fellowship with our Holy Father?

Scripture Reference:

Luke 14:7–11; 18:9–14	Matthew 18:21–22	Hebrews 10:22
Matthew 23:1–12	2 Corinthians 7:1	2 Timothy 1:3
2 Corinthians 11:7	Romans 15:4	1 Peter 2:19
Philippians 4:12; 3:21	Psalm 19:12–13	Psalm 103
1 John 1:8–10	Proverbs 10:12	1 Corinthians 6:19
Proverbs 28:13	Matthew 5:28–30	2 Corinthians 6:16
Ecclesiastes 7:20	Mark 9:43–48	1 Corinthians 2:11–12
Matthew 7:1; 5:23–25; 6:6, 12–15	Romans 12:9–10; 13:8–10	John 6:63
Romans 7:14–20	James 3:2–12, 17; 5:20	
	1 Peter 4:8	

NECESSITY OF SUFFERING

(96) The most perplexing part of the Christian's life is that of suffering. Members of the body of Christ are called to suffer. It is that invaluable, unique ingredient that enhances spiritual maturity. Suffering is closely related to love and obedience. Jesus Christ tasted death for every man's sins because he loved. His great sufferings earned him great rewards. Among other things, God his Father crowned him with glory and honor and gave him a name that is above every name. All mankind is destined for tribulations, afflictions, catastrophes, distresses, perils of the world, various kinds of losses, and disappointments. Some Christians are also delivered unto death and others suffer in their body, so that the life of Jesus may be manifested in their mortal flesh. When Christians yield to suffering, death works in them as an exceeding weight of glory, and life works in those who benefit from their suffering.

(97) As Christ suffered in the flesh, believers are to arm themselves with the same mind. As Jesus endured his cross, despising the shame, believers take up their cross and follow in his steps. As Jesus feared God, he learned obedience and was made perfect through sufferings, and so do believers.

It is when we know Jesus and the power of his resurrection and the fellowship of his sufferings (being made conformable unto his death) that we shall attain unto the resurrection of the dead to serve God in power. In sufferings, God our Maker works in us, sanctifies us, and makes of us another vessel of honor that is pleasing to him. This process renders us fit and prepared for the Master's use.

(98) When tried in the refiner's fire and furnace of affliction and cleansed with washing, believers will come forth as gold. When tempted and their faith is tried, the testings bring about patience and perfection. Christians should not be ashamed, but should glorify God. The time has come that judgment must begin at the house of God, and the righteous shall scarcely be saved. The church is destined to be prepared by God to conform to his intentions and eternal purposes.

(99) Moses exhibited faith and love when he chose to suffer affliction with the people of God rather than enjoy the pleasures of sin for a season. He esteemed the reproach of Christ greater riches than the treasures in Egypt, which he forsook; and he endured, as he saw him who is invisible.

It is better to suffer for doing well than doing evil. We are to lay aside every weight that we carry and the sin that impedes us and to run the race that is before us. The disparity is that Jesus suffered unjustly and we justly. Chastening is not joyful, but grievous; nevertheless, it produces the fruit of righteousness in us, which precedes holiness.

And let us be diligent unless we despair, become bitter, and deprive ourselves of the grace of God. As Jesus, himself, was tempted, he is able to sustain those who are tempted.

(100) When believers yield to God to be lovingly crushed as a fragrant flower, they become unto God a sweet savor of Christ. The Lord chastens those he loves and he scourges those he receives.

Before the foundation of the world, Jesus listened to his Father. After receiving his instructions to sacrifice his life for us, Jesus did not rebel. He did not decline or retreat, but he set his face firmly to do as God commanded. He knew that he would triumph, for God was with him to help him to the end.

In his passion and the days of his flesh, the Son of Man offered up prayers and supplications with strong crying and tears unto God, who was able to save him from death. He was heard by God, as he feared, lest he would disappoint or disobey his Father. Though he was the Son, he learned obedience through suffering. He became the captain of our salvation, was made perfect, and fulfilled his commission. We were made perfect in Christ. Like Jesus, we also obey God when we are also hated, despised, and scorned by many. These we are to love and to these we do good with help and favors, seeking nothing in return.

(101) Christ suffered for us in the flesh. We are to prepare and arm ourselves likewise to follow in his footsteps. All who live godly in this world shall suffer tribulations and be persecuted for righteousness's sake. Believers are reproached, reviled, and spoken of falsely as evil doers. They are denied, rejected, sorrowful, and forsaken as was Jesus. They may have foes within their own household. While believers endure such things, they are reminded to rejoice and be exceedingly glad, for great is their reward in heaven. Disciples of Christ will be hated by the world and by all men, according to the Scriptures, for they hated Jesus before they hated them.

Jesus was exposed to the world and put to shame openly. He rejected comfort, ease, protection, and shelter from this evil world. He was rich, but became poor for our sake. He was meek and lowly. Jesus, our model, left us his examples to follow.

(102) Our merciful God comforts us in all our tribulation so that with this same comfort we may be able to comfort those who are in any trouble. Paul and company encountered so much trouble that they were burdened beyond measure, above strength, and even despaired of life. They had the sentence of death in themselves so that they were reminded not to trust in themselves but in God who raises the dead. Paul confessed, furthermore, that God delivers, God did deliver, and they trusted that God would deliver in the future.

(103) When fiery trials come to try us, we should not think of them as strange things that are happening to us, but rather we are to rejoice, inasmuch as we are partakers of Christ's sufferings. When reproached for the name of Christ, we are to be happy and exceedingly glad. When we are

persecuted, God rests upon us, God is glorified, and we have great reward awaiting us in heaven.

(104) We are troubled on every side; we are distressed, persecuted, and cast down; we are perplexed. On the other hand and to the contrary, we are neither distressed, nor in despair, nor forsaken, nor destroyed. This reveals the glory and power of God in earthen vessels. We bear in our body the dying of the Lord Jesus so that the life of Jesus might be manifested. We are always delivered unto death for Jesus' sake that, again, the life of Jesus might be manifested in our mortal flesh. For this cause we do not faint. Though our outward man perishes, our inner man is renewed day by day. This light affliction, which is only for a moment, works for us a far more exceeding and eternal weight of glory. We do not consider the visible things that are temporal, but the invisible things that are eternal.

(105) Those who are called to suffer know that all things work together for good for those who love God and are called according to his purpose. God predestinated us to be conformed to the image of his Son, that he, Jesus, would be the firstborn of many children of God. Believers are also justified and glorified by God, our Father.

The Word of God declares that the whole creation groans and travails in pain due to the bondage and corruption of the flesh. Even believers groan within waiting for the redemption of our body, the end of our salvation, to the praise of God's glory.

(106) Trials, troubles, losses, sorrows, bereavement, offenses, tribulations, and perils will surely come, but God promises not to leave us nor forsake us. God says that he will not allow our foot to be moved; that he will keep us and not slumber. Temptations are common to mankind, but God will not allow us to be tempted above that which we are able to bear. He will make a way for us to escape, but we must take that way. When we suffer according to the will of God, let us commit the keeping of our soul unto him as our faithful Creator. And let us be persuaded, as Paul, that God is able to keep that which we have committed unto him against that day.

(107) It is wise to do for others all we can when we can. Eventualities occur that we do not understand, unless God gives us the answers. One instance may be the grief and sorrow of losing a dear loved one. We may not comprehend death in this life; however, we may receive consolation in knowing that God gave us the pleasure of their company for a time; that God is love; that he knows best; that his ways are past finding out; that all souls belong to God; that God works all things according to the counsel of his own will and for our good. Another perplexity we may suffer is unexpected financial loss, but we depend upon God and his Word. This, too, is for our benefit. As only God can do, this may be his way of eradicating a tendency to become covetous, which is idolatry.

When we ask God and he shows us the reason and we accept it, we will rejoice and be glad. We will count the loss as a great and profitable blessing rather than regret it as a misfortune. We will not despair, because we will understand that this is for our learning, for our spiritual growth, and for preparation for service to God.

(108) Another kind of suffering that is difficult to understand is when we are persecuted for righteousness's sake: rejected, ostracized, betrayed, despised, reviled, and falsely accused. When persecuted we are to do good to our accusers and wrongdoers, lend and expect nothing in return, provide for them, bless them and pray for them.

It pleased God to bruise his only begotten Son and put him to grief. God was satisfied to see the travail of his soul to pay for the sin of the world. For this, Jesus was given all power in heaven and in earth.

We deny ourselves and become more obedient; we abandon all the things of this world. The greater the abandonment, the greater the power of God in us; the greater the service, the miracles, the blessings, and eventual rewards and glory.

(109) Knowing our destination, that here we have no continuing city, we never look back, because we seek the one to come, the holy city, new Jerusalem. (See Heb. 13:14; Rev. 21:2; Col. 3:1.) Abraham looked for a city whose builder and maker is God. (See Heb. 11:10.) It helps us to not only

have the mind of Christ, but also to accept the mind of Paul. He was regarded as both honorable and dishonorable; of having both good report and evil report; as being unknown, yet well known; sorrowful, yet always rejoicing; poor, yet making many rich; as having nothing, yet possessing all things.

He pressed toward the mark for the prize, and this prize is the high calling of God in Christ Jesus. Suffering is God's way of life for believers and so is love. Love vanquishes all. Glory to God forever.

Scripture Reference:

Philippians 2:5–11;
   3:8–11
Hebrews 2:9–10
1 Peter 4:1–2
Hebrews 5:7–9
1 Peter 2:21–23
2 Timothy 2:12, 20–21
1 Corinthians 4:10–12,
   16–18
Matthew 10:36
John 15:18, 25
Micah 7:6
Jeremiah 18:4–8
Hebrews 6:4–8; 10:26–27
Malachi 3:2
Job 23:10
Isaiah 48:10
James 1:2–4
Proverbs 27:21
1 Peter 4:19

Mark 14:36
John 5:30
Matthew 26:39
Hebrews 11:24–27;
   12:1–29
2 Timothy 2:12
2 Corinthians 4:6–18
Romans 8:18–39
Hebrews 2:18
2 Corinthians 1:1–11
1 Peter 4:12–18
Matthew 5:10–12;
   5:38–42
Hebrews 5:7–9
Isaiah 50:4–9
1 Peter 2:21
Luke 17:1
Psalm 121:3
Hebrews 13:5
1 Peter 4:19

2 Timothy 1:12
Luke 12:15
Isaiah 53:7–12
1 Peter 3:18
Matthew 5:39–42
2 Corinthians 12:9–10
1 Corinthians 10:10
John 15:1–5
Philippians 3:7–15
2 Corinthians 2:15–16
1 Peter 1:7–9
Colossians 2:15
Matthew 11:29
Acts 9:16
Genesis 3:15
John 8:44
Acts 13:10
1 John 3:8
Matthew 13:38
2 Corinthians 6:8–10

Chapter 8

ETERNAL LOVE

And thou shalt love the Lord thy God with all thy heart, and with all thy soul, and with all thy mind, and with all thy strength: this is the first commandment. And the second is like, namely this, Thou shalt love thy neighbor as thyself. There is none other commandment greater than these.

—**Mark 12:30–31**

We love him, because he first loved us.

—**1 John 4:19**

[Jesus said,] If ye love me, keep my commandments.

—**John 14:15**

[Jesus said,] By this shall all men know that ye are my disciples, if ye have love one to another.

—**John 13:35**

Beloved, let us love one another: for love is of God; and every one that loveth is born of God, and knoweth God. He that loveth not knoweth not God; for God is love.

—**1 John 4:7–8**

Hereby perceive we the love of God, because he laid down his life for us: and we ought to lay down our lives for the brethren.

—**1 John 3:16**

And now abideth faith, hope, charity [love], these three; but the greatest of these is charity.

—**1 Corinthians 13:13**

INVINCIBLE LOVE

(1) The church's spiritual condition is dependent almost entirely on one thing—love. Love governs all work and activities of the church. The love of God in our lives is key. God's love abides forever in the heart of believers, who are known by their love. Only in love can the church truly complete its high calling, its mission, and its ministry. The church must allow God's Holy Word to teach them the all-encompassing attributes of love to be found nowhere else. God's love is perfected in those who keep his Word.

The Bible tells us also that we know that we are in God when we walk in love and are set in motion by love. Then the world, starving for love, will no longer wait for the manifestation of God's love in us.

LOVE'S COMMAND

(2) Love is the cardinal thing. It is the first and greatest commandment. Love is the greatest virtue and power. God is love. God's love was demonstrated in the greatest gift to mankind when God gave his only begotten Son to die to atone for sin. Jesus responded in love and obedience to his Father. He fulfilled the law of commandment and paid for the

sins of every person who has or ever will live. Love is not an option for followers of Jesus.

(3) For love and because of love, the Word (God) left heaven, came to earth, which he created, and took upon himself flesh and blood. Jesus became sin for everyone as a substitute for sins, while he knew no sin and could do no sin. The price Jesus paid demanded the most brutal and greatest mutilation of his body that is known to man. For love, it pleased God to put Jesus to grief; and God saw the travail of the soul of his Son and was satisfied that he completed the task.

GENUINE LOVE

(4) If we love Jesus, we will keep his words. Then Jesus and the Father will love us and will come unto us and live with us. When we obey him and keep his commandments, Jesus says we will abide in his love, even as he has kept his Father's commandments and abides in his love. He that dwells in love dwells in God. Love is the bond of perfection.

(5) Our love of God compels us to obey him, unquestionably, without reservation or hesitation. The woman at the well immediately left her water pot and went into the city and told others of Christ. Many of the disciples, whom Jesus called, instantly left whatever they were doing and followed Jesus. In love and obedience, they were willing to do as Jesus commanded. Jesus explained that none of those who are called, but use excuses and disobey, shall taste of his supper at the marriage supper of the Lamb. Those who have ears to hear take heed and put Jesus first in obedience and in every way.

(6) Our love reveals our true motives and sincerity. Love is without hypocrisy. Love is powerful and strong. It covers a multitude of sins. The proof of our love is when we obey God, keep his commandments, and love our neighbor as ourself. Love and obedience are inseparable and mutually exclusive.

LOVE'S TESTS

(7) The holy, eternal Word is very specific in informing, as well as admonishing us, of what love is and what love is not; what love does and does not do. God gave and Jesus gave love. We love and, therefore, we give in love.

Whoever does not love does not know God, says the Word of God, for God is love. We love God because he first loved us and put within us the ability and capacity to love. By this measure we know that we have been saved: Whoever loves his brother has eternal life, because he that loves God loves his brother also. We cannot love God without loving our neighbor, for this is the proof, the evidence, that we love God. God's incomparable love excels man's natural love. The heart is deceitful above all things and desperately wicked beyond our understanding. Love of neighbor is so vital that it defines our relationship with God. The second commandment is like unto the first. They are mutually exclusive.

(8) There are other crucial tests of genuine love. Those who exercise spiritual gifts—such as great faith, unknown tongues, and prophecy—and those who cast out demons and do many wonderful works without love, they do so in vain. The Bible says that these persons are nothing. One may feed the poor with his wealth, or one may do the ultimate—give their life for another. Jesus tells us that such actions, even though done in his name, but done for any reason other than for love have no merit whatsoever. Love commands that believers do not love the world, neither the things that are in the world.

For those who love the world, the love of the Father is not in them. Friendship with the world is enmity against God, and that person is an enemy of God.

VIRTUAL LOVE

(9) Ministry and good works must be motivated by love from the heart, and both demand self-denial and humility. Man loves to do whatever comes

naturally. The Scriptures warn that no person who engages the works of the flesh under such circumstances is justified in the sight of God.

(10) One who loves suffers much. He endures trials, tribulations, and all things though not understanding them. He believes all things, trusting God. He is very patient, kind, and hopeful. He rejoices in the truth, not in iniquity. One who loves does not envy. He is neither proud nor arrogant. He does not behave with corrupt manners, and he is not easily provoked into becoming angry.

LOVE IS ETERNAL

(11) Charity (love) never fails. It endures forever. It is greater than faith or hope, although all three abide forever. The opposite is true of spiritual gifts that have been given to the church for a time and purpose and are temporary and limited. The end of time shall also be their end, because they shall cease and vanish away and be replaced with that which is perfect and eternal in glory.

A FRUIT OF THE SPIRIT

(12) God is glorified when believers bear fruit, which comes by love, a fruit of the Spirit. The church edifies itself through love. The body of believers is to be rooted and grounded in love, the rich spiritual soil, so that the body may effectively grow up into Christ, its Head.

LOVE LOST

(13) The prophetic Word of God says that in these last days iniquity would abound, because the love of many would grow cold. The love of

money, the root of all evil, is rampant and accelerating with all speed. Believers and churches have left their first love (Jesus) for temporal mammon.

Love is the fulfillment of the law. He that loves God and does good is of God. The rich young ruler was deceived by his riches. A certain rich man, who laid up treasures for himself, did not live long enough to enjoy them. The Bible states that those who are rich toward God love their neighbor and give to the poor.

UNSURPASSED LOVE

(14) Love is the cure for all that ails the church. It is at the foundation of the church's very conception.

Jesus had already prayed to his Father that the same love that his Father had for him would also be in us, his own. The depths of the love of God and of Jesus to mankind resulted in believers becoming children—sons and daughters of God and brothers and sisters of Jesus. God's most amazingly profound act of love consummated in our spiritual union with Christ. Believers are a part of the body of Jesus and of his flesh and bones. God chose believers in Christ before the foundation of the world to be holy and without blame before him in love and to be for the praise of his glory in his matchless grace toward us.

(15) Love is the reason why Life, himself, became God's sacrificial Lamb. Love inspires believers to present their bodies as a holy living sacrifice to God and become his servants. The Word of God teaches that believers ought to lay down their life for the brethren, mainly in the spiritual, though sometimes in a real sense.

Love was demonstrated when Jesus came to us meek and lowly. He humbled himself and became God's servant. He was made a little lower than the angels, was fashioned in the likeness of sinful man, and descended into hell for man.

Love was demonstrated when Abraham obeyed God's voice and proceeded to slay Isaac, his only son, for a burnt offering. Abraham put his love of God first, and God rewarded Abraham by sparing his son's life and making him a father of many nations, and a blessing to all nations.

GOD'S LOVE TRANSCENDS KNOWLEDGE

(16) It is time to love and to manifest the love that comes from God. Believers may actually feel God's love in the most intimate way. At a time of God's choosing, he will shower this heavenly bliss upon us, in us, and through us. Such a wonderful experience, no doubt, would lack adequate description in any language.

Love abounding in the whole heart is the gauge that determines the church's spiritual condition and readiness for biblically sound action. Parallel with love is obedience. These two qualities are indispensable to church works and ministry.

When rooted and grounded in love, the church may be able to comprehend the breadth, length, depth, and height and know the love of Christ which passes knowledge. The well-grounded church shall be filled with all the fullness of God. This is the promise of God. The love of Christ that passes knowledge may be to the extent that he suffered in his flesh body sin, sickness and diseases of every person who has or every will exist. Also, it may be to the extent of the fact that believers are made to be a part of Christ, himself, who is God. Love propels sacrificial action, the energy of our faith.

(17) Love commands self-denial, sacrifice, and giving of one's substance. We have the chance in one lifetime on earth to fulfill the

commandment to love. A great vacuum exsits for lack of love. And, regrettably, too many believers are oblivious of the marvelous privilege to please God and love our neighbor.

When we truly love, we are neither distant from God nor arrogant nor indifferent toward those in our surroundings. We are concerned and caring rather than skeptical, suspicious, and disparaging of others. God's love is unbiased and without exemptions or exceptions. Those who love seek out and embrace those who are ostracized, hated, shunned, despised, outcast, needy, abandoned, ignored, and neglected. Deep regret does not compensate for the priceless lost opportunity of the present to choose and to render unexcelled love and compassion to despairing humanity. This is the love of God!

(18) In the next segment of this book, God gives us his specific, extensively detailed plan of action for the church. This is God's admonition and call for the church, individually and collectively, to repent, receive his instruction, and go on to perfection. This is God's initiative to revive, renew, and restore the church to be the church that is structured, functioning, and operating in accordance with his holy, eternal desire, design, plan, purpose, will, Word, and work before the foundation of the world. Love is a condition of revival of the church that has been prepared by God and is now ready for launching by the church. Obedience to God is the evidence of love of God.

Scripture Reference:

Mark 12:30–31
2 Corinthians 5:14
Ephesians 6:24
1 Timothy 1:5
1 Corinthians 11:24–26;
   13:1–13
Galatians 5:21
Isaiah 53:10–11
Ephesians 5:30
John 1:12, 29
Galatians 3:26
1 John 3:1–2

Genesis 3:15
John 14:20–24; 15:8–10
Colossians 3:14
1 John 5:3; 4:8, 16, 21;
   3:14–18
Matthew 24:12
1 Timothy 6:10
Ephesians 1:4–6; 4:15–16
John 17:24, 26
Ephesians 3:16–19
John 3:16; 14:6
Romans 12:1–2

Colossians 3:5
Matthew 20:26; 23:11
Jeremiah 17:9
Ephesians 3:16–19
1 John 2:15
James 4:4
Deuteronomy 6:5, 11:1
Psalm 31:23
Matthew 22:37–40; 7:12
Romans 13:9–10
1 John 4:7–12, 19–21

Chapter 9

THE MYSTERY—ONE CHURCH REVEALED IN THE LAST DAYS

This is a great mystery: but I speak concerning Christ and the church.
—Ephesians 5:32

Now ye are the body of Christ, and members in particular.
—1 Corinthians 12:27

For we are members of his body, of his flesh, and of his bones.
—Ephesians 5:30

So we, being many, are one body in Christ, and every one members one of another.
—Romans 12:5

And he is the head of the body, the church: who is the beginning, the firstborn from the dead; that in all things he might have the preeminence.
—Colossians 1:18

When he ascended up on high, he led captivity captive, and gave gifts unto men. . . . And he gave some, apostles; and some, prophets; and some, evangelists; and some, pastors and teachers; For the perfecting of the saints, for the work of the ministry, for the edifying of the body of Christ: till we all come in the unity of the faith, and of the knowledge of the son of God, unto a perfect man, unto the measure of the stature of the fullness of Christ: That we henceforth be no more children, tossed to and fro, and carried about with every wind of doctrine, by the sleight of men, and cunning craftiness, whereby they lie in wait to deceive; But speaking the truth in love, may grow up into him in all things, which is the head, even Christ: From whom the whole body fitly joined together and compacted by that which every joint supplieth, according to the effectual working in the measure of every part, maketh increase of the body unto the edifying of itself in love.

—Ephesians 4:8; 11–16

And are built upon the foundations of apostles and prophets, Jesus Christ himself being the chief cornerstone; In whom all the building fitly framed together groweth unto an holy temple in the Lord.

—Ephesians 2:20–21

For other foundation can no man lay than that is laid, which is Jesus Christ.

—1 Corinthians 3:11

How that by revelation he made known to me the mystery; (as I wrote afore in few words, Whereby, when ye read, ye may understand my knowledge in the mystery of Christ) Which in other ages was not made known unto the sons of men, as it is now revealed unto his holy apostles and prophets by the Spirit.

—Ephesians 3:3–5

HYPOTHESIS

(1) Throughout this book, the only true God reveals himself and exposes the only one, holy, true church. What the church is and is not are

contrasted. The true church is eternal, spiritual, invisible, active, and alive. The opposite of the true church is a visible, temporal entity without life that operates carnally. The answer is: the revelation of the church of Jesus Christ.

THE END OF TIME AND LAST DAYS

(2) For ages, wars and rumors of wars rage on and on. Who cannot but observe continuous alarming dangers, troubles, catastrophes, perils, and calamities that are dominant throughout the earth? Massacres and carnage are relentless. Rare diseases, pestilences, AIDS, the extremely vexing invisible leeches called dust mites, and many more perplexities are prophetic. Although microscopic, the mites are extremely powerful. Their numbers seem infinite and invincible. They primarily penetrate and inhabit the vulnerable. The mites may possibly be compared to the scorpion, which the Bible says strikes at men, torments, and stings them.

The extreme torment of the intractable, previously unheard of mites of these last days shows a parallel to the everlasting hell that Jesus spoke of, where the fire is never quenched and the worm does not die. Besides all these adversities, there are many anti-christs, false prophets, teachers, and deceivers who would deceive the very elect of God if it were possible. "And no marvel; for Satan himself is transformed into an angel of light" (2 Cor. 11:14). Truth is a rarity, and justice has failed. Peace has been taken from the earth. Blood flows profusely in streets, highways, and byways. Terror and fear, dread and panic persist. The most atrocious, demonic mayhem is occurring with great frequency and speed, because the devil knows that he has only a short time before being bound. Jesus warned that in these last days there would be wars and rumors of wars and great tribulation such as has never been nor shall ever be. He said that unless these days are shortened, no flesh would survive, but for the elect's sake, they would be shortened. The remaining days are, indeed, shortened and speedily coming to a close.

(3) The Bible speaks of the end of this age in words as: the last time, last days, the end is at hand, the Lord is at hand, the coming of the Lord draws near, and end of the world. Fulfillment of prophecy reveals that there is no time left for believers to consider delay or procrastination in unbelief. This is the precious moment to believe and obey God.

(4) The church plays a phenomenal part in these final days, but enormous correction and preparation are absolutely compulsory.

God announced the one and only church in the book of Genesis that continued to unfold throughout the Word of God to the book of Revelation. Jesus delegated to the church, his body, the responsibility to finish the work that he began. This is the final hour, the only chance for the church to act.

(5) As recorded in the four gospels, at the appointed time, Jesus chose from among his disciples twelve apostles and prophets to be the only authentic foundation upon which the church would be established, expanded, and mature. The book of Acts records the birth of the church and beginnings of its powerful work to be done throughout the world. The personal work during the lifespan of the original apostles practically concluded with John on the Isle of Patmos. Jesus gave John the revelation that God gave to him to show to his servants things which must shortly come to pass. God reveals the end of all things existing from the beginning of time. After all enemies have been destroyed, God will create a new heaven and a new earth wherein dwells righteousness.

(6) Time is very short and the hour has come for the church to respond to God's command for restoration. Preparation, change, and action are required. God will instruct the church to know who she is and is not and what her purpose and work is and is not. This is the church's once-in-a-lifetime opportunity, its greatest challenge, and its number one priority.

WHO THE CHURCH IS NOT

(7) The Apostle Paul, who taught, nurtured, and disciplined the church, lamentably prophesied and warned the church of its future spiritual decline. The church began straying from the truth almost as soon as she was born. Eventually, vying for power over the centuries brought about persecutions, executions, martyrs, and the rise and fall of both powers and dogmas. Skeptics, agnostics, heretics, and apostates no doubt stirred the ensuing reformation endeavors. Unfortunately, this led to unbiblical separations and divisions. The martyr of Christians might be much less common today, but disunity is prevalent and continues to multiply.

(8) The deficient church of past and present generations has taken on many forms, demonstrating its nonconformity to the Word of God. Many believers may be surprised to learn or realize that universal designation, acceptance, and practice of the church of clergy and laymen is totally unbiblical. Neither is the church a secular, religious, or denominational organization. Likewise, the church is not a group of congregants that operates according to its own charter, traditions, creed, doctrines, commands, directions, or any other carnal or worldly standards, based on their own prerogative.

(9) The church is not a part of the world. It has no resemblance to and cannot be identified with the world. It is not a friend to the world. Leaders do not make disciples or followers of themselves or their beliefs and philosophies.

Desires of the world are not desires of the church. Being in the world does not diminish and obscure the church's obligation to truth, spirituality, and holiness. The church of Jesus Christ and of God cannot change from its original embodiment. It is not a gathering place for spectators.

(10) The church is not composed of splinter groups—great or small—initiated to embrace different and contrary doctrines. Distinct demarcation exists to imply that the one is correct, the other is in error, and

the chasm is fixed. The church is not a gathering of people who practice and instill controversial doctrinal convictions. It does not organize, promote, advertise, or market programs and agendas that satisfy worldly ambitions of power, prestige, prominence, or monetary gain. Holy Scriptures reveal that there are no politicians, entrepreneurs, financiers, artistic performers, entertainers, or any such deviations that are a part of or a function of the church.

Who is not the church? The church is not composed of people separated by what they call their faith, and consider it one among other different faiths. These faiths, supposedly, are identified as denominations and, perhaps, other religions, but all are unbiblical labels. The Bible confirms that there is only one faith and that is the faith of the gospel of Christ, which is the power of God unto salvation to everyone that believes. Faith is a living experience of spiritual transformation from a state of sin and death to everlasting life through Jesus Christ. Faith is not transferable by any other, whether person or institution.

(11) God cannot fail or be hindered. God saves souls and he never abandons his own, in spite of the church's monumental divergences. The church is not hopeless, but shall be revived. God's end time vision and revelation unveils the mystery of the church in inexhaustible detail for this very purpose. The next segments give the evidence.

FIRST CALL

(12) God has been revealing the revival of the church to many believers during at least the last two decades. Those who are vigilant must surely recognize the overwhelming need. It seems that hearers have been contented with prophesies and with waiting for God alone to bring it to fruition. Repentance comes before revival, just as repentance comes before salvation. God does not come short and needs no repentance. The church is obstinate and in default. God is waiting for the church to repent

of indifference, disobedience, and inaction. It is apparent that God's call is neither truly heard, nor seriously considered, nor vigorously pursued for further clarification, word, and direction. Only God knows when and for whom all opportunity is lost.

(13) Jesus will come quickly. The believer's delay to prepare for this unparalled, unprecedented event is equal to unbelief. God has allowed believers more than enough time to answer to God and get ready. Those who wait hoping to actually see the evidence with their own eyes could be sadly disappointed that their blindness remains and their fate is sealed. Jesus will come at a time when least expected. He is coming again the second time for the church that he formed during his first advent. It will be perfect. It will be flawless. It will be holy.

(14) God showed his mercy and lovingkindness to the Israelites in their comatose state when he commanded Ezekiel to prophesy to the whole house of Israel and Judah. Then God breathed on them (depicted as dry bones) and they became alive again for God's purpose. God's proposal to Ezekiel was that, if he believed the bones could live, to prophesy to them and he would cause breath to enter into them and they would live. Prophecy was fulfilled and there came a noise and a shaking and the bones came together—bone to bone, then sinews and flesh. Ezekiel obeyed God and prophesied again. Then God breathed on the skeletons and they lived and stood up and became an exceedingly great army. God said to them that he had opened their graves and would put his Spirit in them and place them in their own land. They would no longer be Israel and Judah, Joseph and Ephraim—two nations of a divided kingdom. God said he would also write his law within their heart, abolishing the requirement to keep the law through fleshly means.

(15) Under the New Covenant, God again shows his mercy to the Jews in a mystery for a specific purpose. This mystery reveals that because of his mercy shown to the Israelites, the Gentiles also receive mercy. That mercy demonstrated makes eternal salvation obtainable also for the Gentiles.

(16) The great mystery of the church and its revelation also is initiated and unveiled by God to this generation. Understanding the vision requires unwavering belief and obedience to God's commands.

Action by the church assures its awakening and revival, its restoration and complete renewal. This is indispensable to the church that it may perform and finish its preordained work.

(17) The Scriptures profusely sound alarms through instruction, admonition, examples of God's reproof, and punishment. The Lord shall thoroughly purge, refine, and purify his people as in a furnace, and the chaff shall burn with unquenchable fire.

(18) The prophet Isaiah recorded that the people sought to hide from God their resolve and their works in the dark. Since the fear of God was taught by the precept of men, the understanding of their prudent men was hid from them. The unwary said: Who sees us? And who knows us?

(19) Jeremiah said that among God's people were wicked men who spied upon, set traps, and caught indiscreet ones as birds in cages. They deceived men, they shined, and they became powerful and rich. The prophets prophesied falsely and the priests ruled as they pleased. The people loved to have it that way. The people were comfortable and desired no escape from their cages. God said: Shall he not visit them for such things and avenge his soul upon those who do such horrible things? (See Jer. 5:9, 27, 30, 31; 9:9.) And what will these do in the end? Scripture warns believers of the ungodly who are admired by many. They speak great enticing words because of advantage (See 2 Pet. 2:18; Jude 16.) Shall the church of this generation seek to escape from captivity of their own making?

(20) The hand of the Lord was upon Ezekiel, and he went into the sanctuary. He saw great wicked abominations that were done by seventy ancient men of the house of Israel in the house of the Lord. He saw every form of creeping things, abominable beasts, and all of their idols portrayed on the walls. Their backs were toward the temple, their faces toward the east, and they worshipped the sun.

(21) Then God commanded the six men who were in charge of the city to have a slaughter weapon in their hand. He showed them the golden altar. God instructed one of the six men that had an inkhorn to put a mark upon the forehead of those who sighed and cried because they were grieved and saddened by the abominable things done in the house of God.

(22) God said he would not spare, neither have pity, but would repay them for their perverseness and evil ways; for they said, *The Lord has forsaken the earth and did not see.* And so God had these six men begin at his sanctuary and go through the city and slay old and young, even women and children—all except those who had the mark upon their forehead.

(23) Surely, God sees, but who among us sees the abominable things that are happening in the church today? Where are the passionate who are sighing and crying and praying, being grieved and saddened because of the shameful condition of the church today? Who is obeying God's Word and doing his will? And who shall be able to withstand God's judgment that has begun at the house of God?

Who will be ready at the Lord's sudden appearing? In a parable, Jesus exhorted that if an evil servant says in his heart, *My Lord delays his coming, so I shall eat and drink and be drunken,* he shall punish that servant and number him among hypocrites.

(24) Believers of this generation should beware of the fallacies of the church at Laodicea and act according to remedies given by Jesus. They boasted that they were rich, increased with goods, and had no needs. The exact opposite was true. Jesus proclaimed that they were lukewarm, wretched, miserable, poor, blind, and naked. He counseled them to buy from him unperishable gold tried in the fire that they may be rich (truly spiritually rich) and white clothes that they may be clothed (in righteousness and holiness) and not to be ashamed. He advised them to anoint their eyes with eye salve that they may see (be enlightened with truth). If the blind lead the blind, both shall fall into the ditch. God's first call for some could be the last.

REMOVE THE OBSTACLES

(25) The mystery of the church, though plainly written in the Word of God, appears to have been hidden throughout centuries. Blessed are those who have spiritual ears to hear and spiritual eyes to see what the Spirit is revealing to the church. One must wonder why the true identity of the church, ordained by God before the creation of the world, has been undiscernable by believers for such a long period of time. The Word of God and all spiritual things are revealed to believers by the Spirit. It is impossible to understand the spiritual by natural means. Unbelief obstructs discernment.

(26) The veil is upon the complacent believer similarly as it is on the heart of those who disavow the Messiah and embrace Old Testament law. The evidence of obedience is yielding to God until death to carnal flesh. He that loses his life shall save it. God is looking for believers who are dead and their life hid with Christ in God. New wine must be put into new bottles and new cloth is added to new garments. A humble, submissive believer realizes he is nothing, can be nothing, has nothing, and can do nothing without Christ. He is totally dependent on the Father, Son, and Holy Ghost. Such believers are so humbled that they see themselves as being even smaller than a pin dot on the broadest horizon.

(27) The faithful who are purged and cleansed by the Word are prepared to receive and act on God's revelation to the church. They know that to obey God's will, one must be desperate and determined. They are radical, revolutionary, courageous, unrelenting visionaries who are eager, vigorous, and also vigilant. They love the believers and are addicted to ministering to each other. They are obsessed with the things of God. They love the Word of God, are consumed with much prayer, and are soul winners. They are committed and submitted children of God.

THE MYSTERY KINGDOM

(28) As with the church, the kingdom of God is also a mystery. It is within the believer and is, therefore, invisible and intangible. It is not of word, but of power. At the appointed time, the visible kingdom of heaven shall appear on earth.

As described in parables, the kingdom should be as coveted as a hidden treasure in a field or a priceless pearl in the ocean. One then sells all of his possessions to buy them. Those who are hungry for God's great rewards will gladly give up all he possesses to gain all the heavenly kingdom provides.

(29) During his forty days on earth after his resurrection, Jesus spoke about the kingdom of God. His disciples asked him if he would at that time restore the kingdom of Israel. Jesus answered them, saying that it was not for them to know the times and the seasons, which the Father has kept in his own power. The Jewish people knew the history of their earthly kingdom established by God with David as their king, and they yearned for its reinstatement. The prophets Isaiah, Jeremiah, and Micah prophesied concerning the eternal King who was rejected by many. God said he would punish Israel for its waywardness. He would plow them, cut them off, and they would become a worthless heap. Nevertheless, God would show his mercy. Isaiah prophesied the good news, saying that those who sat in darkness had seen a great light that shone upon them. He prophesied that a Son was given and the government would be upon his shoulders.

(30) The kingdom of God cannot be, never has been, and never shall be synonymous with the kingdoms of this world. The heavenly kingdom that is to come on earth is entirely different from the world kingdoms. God raises up all earthly kingdoms and gives them to whomever he pleases. King Nebuchadnezzar learned under excruciating and extremely humbling circumstances that all kingdoms belong to God.

He submitted himself under the mighty hand of God and confessed that the most High God, indeed, rules in the kingdom of men. He acknowledged that God places and appoints earthly kingdoms to whomever he wills. This is God's command of nations until the King comes to end all other rule.

(31) There shall be a new heaven and a new earth, the first heaven and first earth having passed away at the sounding of the last trumpet. Then the kingdoms of this world shall become the kingdoms of our Lord Jesus Christ, who shall reign forever and ever. The holy city, New Jerusalem, shall come down from God out of heaven. The tabernacle of God shall be with men. Jesus said that neither man, nor angels in heaven, nor even he knows the day and hour of that great day, but only the Father.

PREPARE FOR VISITATION

(32) God has chronicled the events of the church from pre-creation, to the prophetic, to its inception through its wavering and its glory. When believers receive God's revival of the church, we will be prepared to perform the greatest, most miraculous works since its beginnings. The church will recall the Scriptures that during Jesus' earthly ministry, many Jews did not recognize him as the Messiah and Son of God. They did not understand that this was the time of their visitation. Jesus said to them that the days would come when they would be severely punished at the hand of their enemies because they did not know the time of his visitation. Jesus wept for the city of Jerusalem. After teaching his disciples, some of them murmured because of what they heard.

They complained that his teachings were hard to understand. From that time, they went back and walked with him no more. Jesus weeps for the church today, because believers are unaware that today is the day and now is the time of his visitation.

(33) The worldliness and immorality that plague the church appears not to be questioned, examined, reproved, or disciplined within the

church. Scrutiny and scathing reports made public are astounding. Scandalous behavior of some said to be affiliated with churches makes them and the church family targets for shameful exposure. That which is done in secret not only comes to light, but is readily spread abroad.

(34) The world must marvel at the church's retrogression, loss of credibility, and unfavorable reputation. Open shame reveals that the church is reduced to the level of a laughingstock, instead of maintaining the stature of holiness with God-given authority and power. This, indeed, is the church's prophetic falling away so that the Son of perdition might be revealed as was Judas Iscariot, a chosen apostle of Jesus.

(35) To believers who truly believe, God makes his vision plain. This is the church's last hour to end its spiritual decline and proceed to a new beginning. Those who receive knowledge of God's revelation to the church are believers who agree with God's reproof, his judgment, and his Word. They confess the truth from the heart that the church virtually has gone from being in a critical condition, to grave, to intensive care, to life support. In familiar language, this typifies the true condition of the church.

The crucial divide is between those who wholly believe God's assessment of the church and those who believe the church is correct, right, and justified in its current state and needs no change, or reform, which is unrealistic.

(36) God calls the church to awake to his voice and respond. Who knows if this is God's last appeal to the church to repent from its downward spiral into the abyss?

(37) Christians should be completely obedient and become immersed in much prayer, fasting, praise, worship, and repentance. We should be eternally grateful for God's visitation. Self-will and self-determination must be entirely surrendered to God. Treasures of earth are to be abandoned for treasures in heaven. Our heart's desire should be that the church vigorously and prayerfully conform to God's Holy Word and will.

THE AZUSA AWAKENING 1906–1924

(38) God has graciously brought about many awakenings and outpourings of his Spirit around the world. The one of greatest magnitude was the Azusa Street Mission revival, which began in Los Angeles, California. Recorded history shows that the believers who were present at these meetings were seeking repentance. They coveted holiness, prayer, true worship, love, humility, and unity for believers in churches universally. Azusa has been compared to a measure of the birth of the church at Pentecost recorded in the book of Acts.

The miracles of the Azusa Street spiritual outpouring that spread worldwide exemplified the power of those that originally occurred on the day of Pentecost. Prayers and supplications to God for revival had been taking place, no doubt, for many years prior by concerned faithful believers, and God graciously answered at Azusa.

(39) That blessed revival at Azusa a little more than one hundred years ago clearly was the most momentous since the birth of the church. It is unfortunate that this event, in only a few years, began to lose its focus on the things so vital in pursuit of complete church revival, restoration, and renewal. Believers desired unity, but this eventually eluded them, due to serious dissentions. The essential church foundation to be established, built upon, and to bring unity never surfaced. Actions taken by individual believers showed that brotherly love also had begun to wane. Accounts of some of the results of this great blessing show that, sadly, some of the errors of previous generations were also repeated. Among the new blessings gained, the invincible baptism of the Holy Ghost and the nine spiritual gifts of the Spirit prevailed and are active today and blessing many.

(40) As this revival grew and became knowledgeable to many, it suffered ridicule and scorn. Different denominations sprang up. The Azusa renewal proved to have come short of expectations. Contentions became commonplace and the movement eventually split into denominations and ethnic groups, the opposite of their hope of coherence. A review of the

records shows that important biblical truths relating to unity were not clearly understood.

The misconception was that the church satisfies the biblical requirement of unity if and when church congregations are made up specifically of believers of all ethnicities and of all nations and cultures. The Bible teaches that true unity is spiritual and is embraced by all believers within the heart that it may be expressed outwardly. True unity is realized through fulfillment of the first and second commandments—love of God first as well as love of neighbor. This precludes despising or rejecting anyone by conforming to customary or worldly practice. Those who have respect of persons are judged by God without mercy, according to the Word of God. Like the kingdom of God, unity also is within. Things not seen are eternal.

(41) Prayers and supplications to God for revival were answered by sending William J. Seymour to the Azusa Street Mission to do a great work. This truly was the prelude to God's impending revival of exceedingly greater proportion.

(42) Records show that William J. Seymour was recognized as the man God used to bring forth the Azusa Revival. Seymour was known as a humble man. He was called a preacher. He did not consider himself higher in rank in the church than other believers, but equal and one with them. He preached holiness and oneness. The meetings were renowned for prayers, and they worshipped and praised God and waited on him.

God answered with salvations, baptisms of the Holy Ghost, various miracles and much more.

RETURN TO THE ONE FOUNDATION

(43) During the Azusa Revival and beyond, the complete restoration of the church was not accomplished, as the most essential component was missing. Believers were unaware at that time, as they failed to recognize that the foundation to build upon was missing. The church's indispensable

true foundation of apostles and prophets with Jesus the chief cornerstone was either unknown, ignored, or incomprehensible. Azusa was direly needed, welcomed, and joyfully received. Since the only true foundation was unrecognized, however, it did not emerge and it remains obscure to this day. For this reason, the church is far off course, being off of its foundation and reduced to chronic mediocrity.

(44) The inevitable church renewal is lingering because its life and action are directly dependent on being on its sole foundation. From the Word of God, there is absolutely no other church foundation except the one that was laid by Jesus Christ. To take a biblical doctrine and attempt to build on it and establish religions, church denominations, sects, or any other organization or foundation is biblically unsustainable and confusing to both believers and unbelievers. If the true foundation consists of only the apostles, prophets and Jesus it does not consist of evangelists, pastors, or teachers, who are certainly a part of the entire body of Christ.

The complete revival of the church cannot occur without the foundation in place. God's imminent revival of this generation completes his great work of Azusa. The church of today shall be built up on its true foundation identical to the church birthed at Pentecost.

(45) God's unprecedented reformation of the church of today begins with the foundation firmly in place. As the Word and revelation of God declares, the foundational support—apostles and prophets—shall be prominently reinstated in the church. This reformation is inevitable.

(46) It is worthy to mention briefly a partial history of the spread of Christianity during the post-Bible era. The modern day church, Catholicism, and the papacy, was founded in Rome. When its authority and probity were questioned, a state of uprisings and persecutions became the forerunner of the great Reformation.

(47) It followed that godly men as John Wycliffe, Martin Luther, John Calvin, John Knox, Roger Williams, John Wesley, and others rose to the forefront. These and others translated the Bible, preached and extolled Scripture,

and Protestantism was born. Realistically, today both Protestants and Catholics continue to hold their positions of separatism. Factions and divisions shall surely vanish with all that is in opposition to God's Word. The Azusa revival produced a token of unity of the body of Christ when believers of Catholic, as well as traditional Protestant, churches received the baptism of the Holy Ghost. Typically, many of these believers were called charismatic.

It so happened that they did not begin a completely new denominational group. Mainly, both Catholics and Protestants remained as such in their own churches.

(48) God has initiated revival and restoration of the one church, the one body of Christ. If we do not believe, God abides faithful. If we deny him, he will deny us. He cannot deny himself.

THE UNVEILED MYSTERY

(49) Understanding the mystery of the church precedes restoration, effective action, and greater works than at any time since the church was born. The body, the church, is a part of the Head, Jesus Christ, the Son of God. Every person who has been or will be born again of the Spirit of God through belief in Jesus Christ is and shall be a member (part) of the body of Jesus, of his flesh, and of his bones. This is a great mystery. Anyone who is not a part of Jesus, likewise, is not a part of the body of Christ. Lack of knowledge leading to nonadherence to this fundamental truth is one important reason why the church is beyond critical but is sustained by God. Knowledge of this union with Christ and with all believers is key to discerning the mystery.

(50) Faith in God and his truths are prerequisite to understanding the mystery. First, the mystery of the church reveals the actual makeup of the body. As the physical body consists of several parts, similarly so does the spiritual body of Christ.

Our physical body visually consists of limbs and faculties, as arms, hands, fingers, legs, feet, eyes, ears, and are made for specific purposes and functions to work harmoniously together. As with the natural so it is with the spiritual body.

(51) The body of Christ consists of parts specifically designed to function according to the purposes of God. Second, God made Jesus to be the Head of the body and the Administrator over all things pertaining to his body, the church. He orders and governs all actions of the body. And third, members of the body are accountable to Jesus. As members are joined to the Head, the whole body works together. Believers (parts) are not independent of one another. No member works separately or is excluded or is nonfunctional. They complement one another. The most phenomenal aspect of the mystery is that each believer is a body part that is an actively functioning ministering gift designated and given not by man, but by Christ. Each minister's gift is placed within the body by God. Each member ministers according to his purpose and function. The whole body of believers is comprised of five parts. They are: apostles, prophets, evangelists, pastors, and teachers. God has set members in the church assembly in the order of rank or prominence for service and benefit to the entire body. He designated the apostles first, prophets second, the teachers third. After these, God specified miracles, healings, helps, governments and speaking in tongues to operate and serve in the assemblies.

(52) We know that in the natural body, the hand is different from the foot; the eye is different from the ear, though all are vital parts of the body. The hand cannot do the same work as the foot; neither can the hand take the place of any other body part, nor can any one part function as an entire body. Likewise, in the spiritual body all parts (ministering gifts), apostles, prophets, evangelists, pastors, and teachers differ one from the other, but they all function together.

(53) The specific function of each body part (ministry) is explained in the appropriate section of this book, along with descriptions of the spiritual gifts, helps, and governing activities. All complement each other. When

believers are taught the whole counsel of God, they will be able to know exactly their own gift(s). God's Word reveals the purpose and function of each part of the whole body so that all will know the relationship and what each was explicitly designed to do.

(54) God formed, tempered, and balanced the spiritual body, as he did the natural body. If the whole body consisted of only a pastor or an evangelist, this would be only one part each and not a whole body—an abnormality. The vision and revelation of God disproves the widely held misconception of any believer that one member of the body could substitute for the whole body. God requires strict adherence to his Word for immediate reformation.

(55) Apostles and prophets, the church's foundation with Jesus, are endowed with all that is necessary for reform. The church's belief in God's eternal truths, followed by obedience, will liberate the deficient church. This will bring healing and renewal of the church for the glory of God.

(56) The church is instructed to leave the principles of the doctrine of Christ and to go on to perfection. The Word of God explains that repentance from dead works, faith toward God, doctrines of baptisms, laying on of hands, resurrection from the dead, and eternal judgment should certainly have been firmly established. The Word of God also permits that teachings on any of these may continue, if necessary. Believers must examine themselves to determine their willingness to agree with God and to go on to perfection. God required that even Jesus, the author of eternal salvation, be made perfect through suffering.

(57) Do we actually believe God and his Word? Are we concerned about the woeful state of the church? Do we fear God? Do we love and trust God? If so, we will do God's will without hesitation or delay. We should not regard God's Word as hard to understand or impossible to perform. We should be of full age consuming strong meat and teaching others. Instead, many are as infants, remaining on milk and who need to be taught the first principles and oracles of God. The revival of the church is inevitable and imminent as we align ourselves with God's Word.

(58) The church will arise when she becomes the house of prayer, with hour upon hour of continual abundant fervent prayer. The one body will emerge when it is in agreement, of one accord, one mind, one speech, one faith, one hope, and one baptism. Believers must have the same love, the same care, and abide by the same rule. Christ, the Head, and the church, the body, are one Spirit.

ONLY ONE WAY

(59) God had the discretion to choose another way or many ways. The way of God is no secret as it concerns the salvation of mankind. God's way is discernible through the Word of God and the Spirit of God. Jesus is the way, the truth, and the life. The words that Jesus spoke are spirit and life. Holy men of God spoke the Word of God as they were moved and inspired by the Holy Ghost. Jesus taught his Word during his earthly mission. The Word of God is alive and lives forever.

(60) When God exposed his resolve and direction for the revival of the church of this generation, he gave the absolute, precise, irrefutable Scriptures to follow. He provided this one way for the church to be restored and to succeed and prevail. Ephesians, the fourth chapter, verses eight through sixteen, are specific. These Scriptures give the exact purpose, function, and operation mandated for the church. Many other Scriptures also corroborate, clarify, and identify serious nonconformance. These Scriptures prove that when God's Word is perpetually compromised, it is impossible for the church to escape from its frail existence and recover from its abysmal diversion from the truth. God's intervention is our phenomenal gift.

(61) The Word of God designates the various parts of the body of Christ and explains the only way they are designed to function. If any part is missing or inoperable, it is less than whole and a divergence from the truth.

The only right way for the church to go is to repent and emerge as a whole body to flourish and to finish its preordained work. The Bible says that there is a way that seems right to a man, but the end of that way is death.

(62) God teaches, instructs, and guides us in the way to go on to perfection. That pathway is the way of holiness. God called us with a holy calling to be conformed to the image of his Son. The only way acceptable to God is to follow peace with all men and also holiness, for God says without these no man shall see the Lord. We keep peace with all men—saint or sinner, friend or foe. Jesus, the Prince of Peace, is the Mediator between God and men. Holiness, peace, and love are the ways and the commands of God. Obedience is not without cost and neither is it without great reward.

(63) Faith is the only way to please God. It requires unrelenting trust, resolve, determination, and perseverance. Faith is believing the Word of God that says faith is the substance, the intangible evidence, of the existence of things and answers we seek.

(64) The way to please God is total submission and surrender of our will, ways, plans, and works to God's way designed for us. The ways of the church that are counter to the Word of God, however innocent or sincere, are now exposed.

(65) In the last days of opportunity, the church is urged to press toward the mark for the prize of the high calling of God in Christ Jesus. And Jesus promised to sanctify, wash, and cleanse the church so that she has neither spot, nor wrinkle, nor any such thing.

She shall be holy and without blemish when Jesus shall present his bride, his glorious church, to himself. The most excellent way is provided by God through his Son the Lord Jesus Christ. During his sojourn on earth, Jesus fulfilled every aspect of that way from birth to death. The pinnacle of God's way for believers from birth to death is to fulfill his preordained purpose in us. This is the reason for having lived on earth. Mankind ascribes to many personal desires, preferences, and goals in life.

All of these—no matter how noble—are secondary to God's way. Through it all, we shall greatly rejoice when we realize we have known our purpose for having been on the earth and have accomplished it.

GREATER WORKS

(66) The whole body of Christ: apostles, prophets, evangelists, pastors, and teachers minister within local churches to do greater works than have been done previously. God prepared the body to perform his extraordinary work in these last days. Instruction in sound doctrine will remind the church that Jesus abolished the law and blotted out former ordinances, which were a shadow of things that presently exist. The first material tabernacle of God was replaced with the temple. Both were finally replaced with the body of believers who are the living, breathing temple of God and a part of the body of Jesus Christ. The works of God can be accomplished only by strict adherence to the Word of God and performed by the entire body of Christ.

(67) During his earthly ministry, Jesus performed multitudes of signs, wonders, and miracles in the presence of his disciples that were not reported in their writings. The apostle John said that if every one of these supernatural things that Jesus did were written, the world could not contain the books that should be written.

(68) Jesus has commissioned the church to do even greater things than he did, because his ministry was short in comparison. He is with his Father in heaven as Head and Administrator of the church while the church on earth finishes the work that he began. These works of miracles, signs, and wonders shall be greater in number, as well as intensity.

(69) New Christians shall be exceptionally blessed to be instructed and nurtured in the most perfect way in the revived church. The restructured church of Christ operates according to the New Testament in the

The Mystery—One Church Revealed

Spirit, rather than in the annulled Old Testament law. As the church is restored, new believers can be assured that they shall advance from babes fed on the milk of the Word to matured teachers, having ingested the meat of the Word. They will shun the enticing words of man's wisdom when they see the demonstration of the Spirit and of power. They will learn which gifts and ministries Jesus and the Holy Spirit have given them. They will grow and be edified to the degree of preparedness to answer the call to minister and serve united with members of the body of Christ.

(70) First Corinthians, chapter fourteen gives the divine order for church assemblies to operate and conduct church activity. Any alternatives of man have no legitimacy and circumvent the Word of God. Jesus, the Head, along with apostles and prophets, first rebuild the church on its true foundation. They restore true doctrines, correcting and abolishing all worldly traditional practices and functions. Prophets cry out, blow the trumpet, and sound the alarm with words of admonition, edification, and comfort. Along with evangelists, pastors, and teachers, the church shall be whole again.

(71) God gave precise instructions to Moses for the construction and operation of the temporal tabernacle and temple. In like manner, God has given specific imperatives to the living church. First Corinthians, chapter fourteen gives the divine order for church assemblies to operate and conduct church activity.

When the church comes together, there are miracles, prophesies, speaking in tongues, interpretation of tongues, prayers, music, singing, giving of thanks, teaching, preaching, and other things. All things are done as the Spirit leads the people. One believer will have a prophecy, another a revelation, another a message in tongues, another an interpretation of tongues. All is done for the edification of the members of the body of Christ. Unbelievers may also be present in church assemblies. Speaking in tongues is a sign for unbelievers. Isaiah prophesied that God would speak to his people in stammering tongues, which they would refuse. This is the rest and refreshing that God would send in the last days. Interpretation is required to follow speaking in tongues. Prophetic utterance blesses believers, unbelievers, and the unlearned.

Apostle Paul counseled the Corinthians: "Wherefore, brethren, covet to prophesy, and forbid not to speak in tongues" (1 Cor. 14:39). The pastor, the overseer and under-shepherd, is responsible to see that all things are done decently and in order. He provides sustenance and guidance toward maturity for service. The end is that all ministries (body parts) are active and are not being prone to atrophy or to seek fertile pasture elsewhere.

(72) It is when (not if) the church is revived that its current methods of operation will be abolished. Church failures due to traditional practices will no longer be accepted or tolerated. The renewed obedient church shall be a wellspring for multitudes of salvations, extraordinary miracles, profound revelations, and infinite possibilities through Christ.

(73) During restoration of the church, the most salient errors inherently contrary to biblical doctrines shall be finally corrected. Prominent among these are: tithing, baptisms, sanctification (separation from the world), and the ill-conceived denominationalism. The church shall be able to receive the revelation God gave to his Son to send to his servants. Believers are blessed when they read God's portrayal of both blessed and woeful events that shall shortly come to pass. Zealous believers prepare to receive revelation of these unprecedented events of these final days. The Father worked through his Son. Jesus works through the church, his body, to complete the work that God began before the creation of the world. Four of six seals recorded in Revelation are open. Our work is to be done, even as current horrendous acts and perilous conditions exist. Peace having been taken from earth causes people to kill one another.

Death occurs by weapons, beasts, and hunger. Food, oil, and wine are or shall be at a premium; nevertheless, the oil and the wine are to be spared from harm. Prudent and vigilant believers will be ready for impending events upon the opening of the fifth seal. The Bible says those who read, hear, and remember the prophetic words of Revelation are blessed. Before the end of time, each believer shall be judged by Christ on his works. Some works shall survive this trial by consuming fire and some shall not.

(74) Time shall come to an end. Heaven and earth shall pass away, and God will create a new heaven and a new earth in righteousness. Sin, corruption, violence, and death shall be nonexistent. Presently, we revel in God's glorious sights and sounds of lofty mountain peaks, deep gorges, flowing streams, and vast undulating oceans. We behold the grandeur of the heaven and wonder what lies beyond such brilliance of sun, moon, and stars. God's heavenly treasures of ice and fire, snow, and rain span earth's breadth and length of the perpetual vegetative covering of stately greenery and varicolored brilliance.

(75) God made a superabundance of blessings available for man's pleasure and enjoyment. Words are inadequate to express such kindness, generosity and breathtaking beauty. Far surpassing man's imagination, the Bible says that eye has not seen, nor ear heard, neither has it entered into the heart of man the things God has prepared for those who love him. In the ages to come in the regeneration, God promises to show the exceeding richness of his grace evident in his kindness toward us through Christ.

The church has scarcely appropriated the abundant blessings God has provided for this life. Beyond these, God has reserved for us in heaven blessings unimaginable to the human mind. For believers, this is the reward of God's work and grace.

ALPHA AND OMEGA OF THE MYSTERY

(76) The mystery preceded God's creation of the heaven and the earth. Afterward, when God formed man from the dust of the ground, the body of Christ already existed in Jesus, the Word, before the world was

framed. The Lord Jesus Christ was slain (crucified) before the foundation of the world, and being within him so was the church. Prophecy further disclosed that after his reincarnation by way of his birth, death, and resurrection Jesus would conquer Satan and abolish death. The depths of the love of God and his Son embodies the mystery.

(77) The secret hidden by God through ages and generations is now unveiled and revealed to the saints. Believers were predestined to die and to be made alive together with Christ, being a part of his body, his flesh, and his bones. Man's creation by God in his own image was obscured by the fall of man. God restored believers to be conformed to the image of Christ. God chose this way of all the ways he could have chosen or created to bridge man's alienation from God.

(78) Before his ascension to heaven, Jesus established the church and instructed his disciples to wait for the promised Holy Spirit, who would birth the church into the world—the church that existed in Christ before the world began. God's revelation of the mystery begins with his marvelous call and his blessed hope for the church.

In the interim between Alpha and Omega, thankfully, God's grace is available to all. The end-time revelation of the mystery of God was given to his Son, who sent it to the church. God speaks first to the church, whom he reproves and also prescribes corrigible remedies for all their deficiencies. Then a degree of mayhem and destruction occurs in the earth that never has been nor ever shall be. At appointed times, judgments with eternal punishment are meted out to peoples, kingdoms, the devil, the beast, and the false prophet.

Former things pass away. The mystery of God unfolds further with the sounding of the seventh trumpet. God makes all things new, including a new heaven and a new earth. The bride of Christ attends the marriage supper of the Lamb. The New Jerusalem appears out of heaven. Believers receive their inheritance. Jesus rules and reigns forever! The foregoing is only a partial view of things destined shortly to come to pass, according to the Revelation of God. It is incomprehensible to conceive that even in our mortal existence believers are in Christ, who is in God (John 10:38; 17:21–24). Christ is the image of God, and believers are the image of Christ (Heb. 1:3; 2 Cor. 3:18; Rom. 8:29). This unveiling ends in the phenomenal manifestation that God chose to make redeemed man a part of himself from Alpha to Omega, eternal and everlasting.

Scripture References:

Romans 8:29	*Matthew 24:entire chapter*	*2 Peter 3:7, 10–13*
Ephesians 1:18; 2:5–6	*Philippians 4:5*	*Philippians 3:18*
Colossians 1:26–27; 2:10	*1 Peter 4:7*	*Ephesians 4:5*
Revelation: the entire book	*Mark 9:43–44*	*Philippians 1:27*
Romans 13:11–12	*Isaiah 65:17*	*1 Corinthians 16:13*

Appendix A

THE HOLY SPIRIT AND THE GIFTS OF THE SPIRIT

This dissertation was presented by the author, on April 28, 1998, at a distinguished Bible college.

Good morning. My name is Rubye Edwards. We will be spending the next hour together learning about a very interesting and most important person, and that person is the Holy Spirit, or the Holy Ghost, as he is also called. As an introduction, the title of this lecture is: The Holy Spirit and the Gifts of the Spirit. Our purpose is to get to know the Holy Spirit in a most intimate way and also to understand why we should personally know him. I am sure we all realize that whatever time we have will be insufficient to do justice to such an infinite person, but I assure you that by the end of this discussion, you will have the information you need so that your lives will be totally transformed and greatly enriched. And you will be fired up and inspired to continue to grow in the relationship with the Holy Spirit.

The study of the Holy Spirit is vitally needed today because a great many Christians—whether Spirit-filled or not—lack vital knowledge of this third person of the Trinity. As you may be aware, the subject of the Holy Spirit has been very controversial or even avoided and, historically, has been a concern for a number of denominational churches, as well as individual believers. In the book of Acts, chapter nineteen, verse two, it is recorded that Paul asked the question of John's disciples at Ephesus: "Have ye received the Holy Ghost since ye believed? And they said unto him, We have not so much as heard whether there be any Holy Ghost." It is certainly probable that as we near the twenty-first century, many believers still might answer that question in the same way. Further in that chapter, we read that Paul proceeded to minister to them. He laid hands on them, and they received the Holy Ghost, spoke in tongues, and prophesied.

Over the centuries, believers have advanced in their understanding of the Word of God and of the Holy Spirit and his works. In the church, however, there are still many unanswered questions facing believers individually and the church collectively. During this lecture, we shall endeavor to clarify many of the more common misunderstandings and lack of understanding about the personality of the Holy Spirit and his relationship to each believer. It should not surprise us that in this end time, the last of the last days, there is a heightened interest in the Holy Spirit at a time when God is fulfilling his promise to pour out his Spirit upon all flesh. (See Acts 2:17.)

As a result of this teaching, my hope is that you will have been challenged and equipped to begin and to continue a relentless pursuit to follow after the Holy Spirit in holy fellowship and communion with him, with the Father, and with the Son. We expect that key questions you have about the Holy Spirit will be answered and clarified as you learn:

1) Who the Holy Spirit is,
2) Why you need the Holy Spirit,
3) How to receive the baptism of the Holy Spirit,
4) How to grow in relationship with him,
5) How and why you should pray for spiritual gifts,
6) The value of praying in the Spirit, and more.

It is time to seek the Lord. It is time to know who this Holy Spirit is. A Bible verse we quote so often is Hebrews 11:6: "But without faith it is impossible to please him: for he that cometh to God must believe that he is, and that he is a rewarder of them that diligently seek him." We know that God performs his word, and "Whatsoever we ask, we receive of him, because we keep his commandments, and do those things that are pleasing in his sight" (1 John 3:22). We shall receive the reward of knowing the Holy Spirit when we have faith and obey God. It is written in the book of Acts that God gives the Holy Ghost to those who obey him.

In the first of two parts of the lecture, we will consider the question: Who is the Holy Spirit? And within that context, we will examine the doctrine of the Holy Spirit. This will be followed by a discussion on the work of the Holy Spirit in the church, which is the conclusion of the lecture.

WHO IS THE HOLY SPIRIT?

First and foremost, the Holy Spirit is God. His basic substance is one and the same as that of the divine Father and the Son. As Christians, we know and acknowledge him as the third person of the Trinity, but subconsciously or not, many believers relegate to the Holy Spirit a position of least importance among the three. In the early church, a concept that was developed and taught concerning the Spirit's deity was that the Spirit was equal to the Father in nature and essence, but was inferior to him in rank.

According to the Word of God and in Christian practice, it is perfectly clear that there is no subordinate relation, position, or role of the Spirit in the Trinity. There is a coordinate role. The Holy Spirit exists eternally with the Father and with the Son, who is the Word. It is noted in Genesis: "In the beginning God created the heaven and the earth, and the Spirit of God moved upon the face of the waters" (Gen. 1:1–2). Chapter one, verse twenty-six reads in part: "And God said, Let us make man in our image, after our likeness." The Spirit played a coordinate role, as the incarnate Christ was dependent upon the Spirit's anointing. Isaiah prophesied: "The Spirit of the LORD God is upon me; because the LORD hath anointed me to preach good tidings" (Isa. 61:1). Everything unfolded about the Spirit in the New Testament is already found in the Old Testament, with the exception of the word *baptize*.

The divine objective of the Spirit is to carry out God's provisions in heaven and in earth. The Spirit is said to proceed from the Father: "But when the Comforter is come, whom I will send unto you from the Father, even the Spirit of truth, which proceedeth from the Father, he shall testify of me" (John 15:26). The term, "proceedeth," by no means infers that the Spirit was created by the Father or that this was the Spirit's origin or beginning of existence.

THE DEITY OF THE HOLY SPIRIT

Inasmuch as the Holy Spirit is God and has the attributes of God, he is also deity. Whatever the Spirit does in and for the believer, he does in the manner of deity. He does not merely influence the human heart from without as an angel, but from within as true deity. Deity enjoys living companionship in intimacy and family fellowship.

THE TRINITY—THREE IN ONE

God the Father, Jesus the Word, and the Holy Ghost are each divinely independent while at the same time they are One. They are inseparable. They are united and they cooperate in one accord in all of their functions and activities. An example of oneness: In Isaiah 6:8, the Spirit is recognized as "the voice of the LORD," but this reference when quoted in Acts 28:25 reads in part: "Well spake the Holy Ghost by Esaias the prophet." Hebrews chapter three, verses seven through nine explains that the Israelites protested in the wilderness against the Holy Ghost, while Exodus 17:7 clearly indicates that the Lord was the one who was offended.

We can see that these Scriptures emphasize the fact of oneness of the Triune God. While this is true, it seems to be widely known in the church that the Holy Spirit is the lesser known of the three. The study of the Holy Spirit is not only needed, but is justified, because the New Testament church growth can be attributed to the systematic study and understanding of the Holy Spirit and the acceptance of his person. When the church is able to get this divine relationship into perspective, we will surely go forward in our searching and gain a knowledgeable position and a closer, more intimate relationship with the Holy Spirit.

The most clear, positive, and conclusive statement of the equality and oneness in the Godhead, in my opinion, is given in 1 John 5:7, which says, "For there are three that bear record in heaven, the Father, the Word, and the Holy Ghost: and these three are one."

THE NAMES OF THE HOLY SPIRIT

We can understand the person of the Holy Spirit through his identity with the Father and the Son by the different names ascribed to him as: the Spirit of God, the Spirit of Christ, and the Spirit of the Lord. These terms denote deity and the status of equality within the Trinity. The Holy Spirit is known by many names in the Bible, and these relate to his work and ministry.

The titles of the Holy Spirit do not detract from the Spirit's personality. The designations Spirit of God or Spirit of Christ necessarily complement one another. The Godhead is altogether omnipotent, omnipresent, and omniscient. The Holy Spirit is Christ present in Spirit. He did not take the place of Christ, but from Scripture he may be thought of as a delegated representative rather than a mere substitute. The title Holy Spirit establishes a contrast between his spiritual essence and material substance and distinguishes him from all unholy spirits in the world. In the Old Testament, the Spirit of the Lord is mentioned several times. The Spirit of the Lord came upon men chosen by God for special service; "The Spirit of the Lord came upon David," and upon others, as recorded in the Scriptures.

OTHER NAMES AND TITLES OF THE SPIRIT

Spirit of Truth—"He will guide you into all truth" (John 16:13).

Spirit of Grace—"Hath done despite unto the Spirit of grace" (Heb. 10:29).

Spirit of Adoption—"Ye have received the Spirit of adoption, whereby we cry Abba Father" (Rom. 8:15).

Spirit of Promise—"Ye were sealed with that holy Spirit of promise" (Eph. 1:13).

Spirit of Wisdom—All true wisdom comes from the Spirit, who is wisdom's channel. (See Eph. 1:17.)

Spirit of Life—"The law of the Spirit of life in Christ Jesus hath made me free from the law of sin and death" (Rom. 8:2).

Comforter—There are four biblical references to the Holy Spirit by his title, Comforter, all of them spoken by the incarnate Jesus and recorded in John's Gospel. "And I will pray the Father, and he shall give you another Comforter, that he may abide with you for ever" (John 14:16).

The word, *Comforter*, in the original is the word, *parakletos*, and it appears in its transliterated form as "Paraclete." The word untranslated simply speaks of the Paraclete. Proposed modern synonyms include: instructor, guide, advocate, assistant, helper, caretaker, and attorney. As Paraclete, the Holy Spirit is ready to provide counsel, wisdom, guidance, strength, and grace in all needed ways; he gives battle on behalf of another.

The earthly Comforter looks after Christ's interests in the believer. The Holy Spirit desires to be the believer's warm personal friend. Jesus promised not to leave his people comfortless or orphaned. One outcome of the ministry of the Spirit as Comforter is the growth in numbers and spiritual power of the church of Christ on earth.

Some other titles recorded in Scripture are: Eternal Spirit, Spirit of prophecy, Breath of the Almighty, Spirit of might, Spirit of revelation, and the seven Spirits of God.

SOME ROLES AND OFFICES OF THE HOLY SPIRIT

The Spirit's personality is revealed by his several roles and offices. His roles are sometimes either expressed explicitly or implied. The name Comforter was designated by Jesus, as he said: "I will pray the Father, and he shall give you another Comforter, that he may abide with you for ever" (John 14:16). The Spirit's basic office is that of Comforter. The office of Comforter and the words of Jesus, "another Comforter" definitely entail that of a personality. Other offices and roles that identify his personality are:

- Creator: "And the Spirit of God moved upon the face of the waters." (Gen. 1:2). The Psalmist penned, "Thou sendest forth thy spirit, they are created" (Ps. 104:30).
- Author: He is author of the Scriptures. "All scripture is given by inspiration of God" (2 Tim. 3:16).
- Teacher and Guide: "He shall teach you of all things;" and "He will guide you into all truth" (John 14:26; 16:13).

The offices of the Trinity and each one in particular help to define the person of the Holy Spirit. In 1 Corinthians chapter twelve, verses four through seven, you will find the most interesting and definitive delineation of the general offices, functions, and operations of the Father, Son, and Holy Ghost in relation to the church. The Father is the Operator, Jesus is the Administrator, and the Holy Spirit is the giver and manifestor of spiritual gifts. You should read and study those functions and activities very carefully.

SYMBOLS OF THE HOLY SPIRIT

Throughout the Word of God, the Holy Spirit is described by title, but most symbols of the Spirit are inferred rather than explicitly identified. The symbols of the Holy Spirit represent him as the Third Person of the Trinity in operation and function, and they reveal his character and reflect his nature. The grounds for some of the inferences include parallel language, a specific association, or a descriptive adjective that interchanges the Spirit and the symbol. The symbols describe the function of the Spirit in terms of the function of the symbol. As many as a dozen biblical symbols of the Spirit may be recognized, and some of them may be combined. Job said: "The Spirit of God hath made me, and the breath of the Almighty hath given me life" (Job 33:4).

Wind or Breath. Wind or breath is unseen, but is powerful, life-giving, and refreshing. It symbolizes the redemptive work of the Spirit. Jesus said: "The wind bloweth where it listeth . . . so is every one that is born of the Spirit" (John 3:8).

Fire. Fire breaks down some substances; it consumes, purifies, warms, tests, and generates power. At Pentecost: "There appeared unto them cloven tongues like as of fire, and it sat upon each of them" (Acts 2:3). Since the Spirit is the Spirit of burning, fire is indeed an appropriate symbol.

Water. Water symbolizes a common agent in washing and cleansing. The Spirit purifies from sinful habits and becomes to the soul a refreshing and cleansing fountain.

Seal. The seal, a symbol of the Spirit, was used in biblical times in the same way a signature is used today. Paul said this about the seal symbol: "Now he which stablisheth us with you in Christ, and hath anointed us, is God; who hath also sealed us, and given the earnest of the Spirit in our hearts" (2 Cor. 1:21–22). In Old Testament times, an earnest of a basket of fruit or a handful of wheat would be sufficient to seal a transaction involving a sale of an orchard or a grain field, and this transaction assures the binding contract. Paul assured the Ephesians: "Ye were sealed with that Holy Spirit of promise" (Eph. 1:13). The Spirit as a seal guarantees security as far as God is concerned.

Oil. Oil is used for anointing. As Jesus began his ministry, he proclaimed: "The Spirit of the Lord is upon me, because he hath anointed me to preach the gospel to the poor" (Luke 4:18). Paul testified concerning the believer: "[He which] hath anointed us, is God" (2 Cor. 1:21). Because the Spirit ministers as anointing oil, the believer is legally set apart as king and priest.

Dove. The dove ministry of the Holy Spirit is identified with the earthly life and ministry of the incarnate Christ. Each of the four gospels reports the descent of the dove in the account of the baptism of Jesus.

Among the characteristics of the dove that have application in understanding the Spirit are: gentleness, tenderness, grace, innocence, mildness, peacefulness, patience, and faithfulness. The dove is pronounced ceremonially clean in Scripture, and this agrees with his nature. The dove is selective in diet, swift in flight, beautiful in plumage, gregarious and sociable in manner of life, and monogamous in mating practices.

It is interesting that the first biblical mention of the Holy Spirit depicts him as ministering in a dovelike manner. The Scripture is Genesis 1:2 which states: "And the Spirit of God moved [that is, brooded or fluttered] upon the face of the waters." The Holy Spirit seldom demands or compels. As a dove, he primarily works by gentle leadings and persuasions. He delights in conveying the peace of God.

Clothing. Another symbol, clothing, is that which we put on. The Spirit is one whom the believer must put on, even as the old nature is put off. We put on the armor of light and the whole armor of God. Being clothed, the believer is protected, adorned, and covered.

THE PERSONALITY AND ATTRIBUTES OF THE HOLY SPIRIT

By careful investigation, it can be seen that the characteristics of the Spirit entitle him to be considered personal. A real person is not the physical body, but is the spirit and/or soul within that body. The Spirit operates within the inner being, invisible in form and mysterious in manner. He has all of the attributes of God. Until some scholars began the development of the doctrine of the Spirit's personality, the fact of his personality had been misunderstood, repudiated, and denied.

The Holy Spirit is not an influence. He is not just a power that God uses to carry out his purposes and will in the universe. The Holy Spirit has personal characteristics of intellect, will, and emotions.

The Holy Spirit prays and intercedes for us according to the will of God, who knows the mind of the Spirit. (See Rom. 8:27.) He intercedes for the saints with groanings that cannot be uttered.

The Spirit exercises will: "But all these worketh that one and the selfsame Spirit, dividing to every man severally as he will" (1 Cor. 12:11). This is an independent exercise of will or one's own mind, and this is a distinctive characteristic of personality. Not only does the Spirit choose according to his will, but also, in cooperation with the eternal Godhead, he effects these choices in this universe.

The Holy Spirit has emotions and feelings and he can be grieved. The believer is commanded: "Grieve not the holy Spirit of God" (Eph. 4:30). The Spirit manifests emotions of love and jealousy and can be insulted and quenched. The believer can also resist him and lie to him.

It is very needful for believers to yield to the Spirit, seek to obey him, and develop a desirable relationship with him to the glory of God. The Scriptures say, "Ye know him; for he dwelleth with you and shall be in you" (John 14:17).

Please keep in mind: the Holy Spirit is not to be thought of as a power to be captured and contained in the human, not merely a principle of life, but he is specifically and uniquely a divine person with the character traits and relationships that are appropriate for a person.

OTHER ACTIVITIES OF THE SPIRIT

We have discussed the various works of the Holy Spirit in creation, in anointing and so forth. Some other specific activities, especially as they relate to his personality and his work in people are:

1. He teaches. (Luke 12:12; John 14:26; 1 Cor. 2:13)
2. He speaks. (John 16:13; Rev. 1–3; Acts 1:16)
3. He grieves. (Eph. 4:30; Isa. 7:13)
4. He testifies. (John 15:16)
5. He intercedes. (Rom. 8:26)
6. He reveals. (John 16:13–15; Luke 2:26; 1 Cor. 2:10)
7. He witnesses. (John 15:26; 1 John 5:8; Acts 5:32)
8. He commands. (Acts 10:13–20)
9. He convicts and reproves. (John 16:8)
10. He leads. (Matt. 4:11; Rom. 8:14; Mark 1:24; Eze. 3:14)
11. He empowers. (Acts 1:8)
12. He comforts. (John 14–16)
13. He quickens. (1 Peter 3:18; John 6:63)
14. He guides. (John 16:13)
15. He glorifies Jesus. (John 16:15)

Before going on to the very enlightening subject of the doctrine of the Holy Spirit, let us review briefly:

So far, I hope we have learned that the Holy Spirit is a Person who has a distinct personality. He is God and possesses all of the divine attributes of the Godhead. He is in himself a living, powerful, intelligent Person. He has a mind, a will, and feelings. He convicts people of sin, and he is also gentle.

The Holy Spirit is omnipresent, omniscient, and omnipotent. He is co-equal in the Trinity. He enjoys intimacy, divine companionship, and cooperation in all of the functions and activities of the Triune God.

The names and titles of the Holy Spirit denote his divine character and indicate his role, office, activities, and work as God. We have learned also that fire, water, wind, oil, seal, and dove are biblical symbols of the Holy Spirit that describe his functions.

THE DOCTRINE OF THE HOLY SPIRIT

This next segment on the Holy Spirit involves a study of the doctrine of the Holy Spirit. Christian scholars have compiled very valuable and extremely interesting information on how Christians have viewed the Person of the Holy Spirit over several centuries since Pentecost, or since the early church age. The study of the doctrine of the Holy Spirit is very enlightening, but we will be able to cover only a few highlights.

The doctrine of the Holy Spirit is not abstract theology. To the degree that the Holy Spirit has chosen to reveal himself, he is also meant to be known and understood, because even doctrinal truths are made understandable and alive by the Holy Spirit.

The teachings of Scripture concerning the Holy Spirit are not as numerous as those that concern the Father and the Son. Nevertheless, 88 references to the Holy Spirit may be found in the Old Testament, and 261 in the New. The Spirit is mentioned or alluded to in 22 of the 39 Old Testament Books, and in all Books of the New Testament except Philemon, 2 John, and 3 John. Contemporary Old Testament teachers, writers, and commentators lacked definite information regarding the person of the Holy Spirit. As Griffith Thomas summarizes: "The Spirit is a Divine agent and energy rather than a distinct personality. God is regarded as at work, and, as in the New Testament, the Spirit is the executive of the Godhead. He is not a gift separate from God, but God himself in and with men; a Power rather than a Person."

A study of the writings of men (mostly of the early centuries), such as Pearlman, Herman (AD 150), Justin Martyr (BC 100–165), Cambron,

Arius of Alexandria, Irenaeus, The Ebionites, and The Gnostics, will reveal that there was productive thought as well as arguments and divisions on the subject of the Spirit as a Person. It is clear that many of the writers found the fact of the personality of the Holy Spirit difficult to apprehend. The earliest clear-cut statement of the personality of the Spirit was by Origen (AD 185–254).

In the early church, to much of Christendom, the Holy Spirit was only a name. In the years following, some of the church fathers did concern themselves with the doctrine of the Spirit and developed some significant, though minimal, insights. There were also unscriptural doctrines and outright errors. By the sixteenth century, the Protestant Reformation developed the full doctrine. In the twentieth century, Pentecostals experienced slow or modest development. In the 1960s, however, the rise of the charismatic movement brought sweeping changes.

It is now observed and acknowledged that the doctrine of the Holy Spirit has reached a level of development never before known in the history of the modern church. Many church denominations that formerly opposed and denigrated the baptism of the Holy Spirit and speaking in tongues now embrace the doctrine. From general observations, though, there is still much open admission of opposition by a large number of professing Christians and denominations. There should be concern for the lack of laborers for the harvest field, and there should be concern also for Christians who are unreached as far as the baptism of the Holy Ghost is concerned.

As you no doubt realize, there has been much controversy surrounding the Person of the Holy Spirit. I feel, and I am sure you do also, that we are very blessed to have the privilege to learn more about the Spirit, who is truly our teacher ready and willing to reveal truth.

Research of Bible scholars' commentaries on the person of the Holy Spirit will reveal that some espoused the belief that the Holy Spirit is subordinate to the Father and the Son. According to the Word of Truth, the Word of God, it is indisputably clear that the Father, the Son, and the Holy Ghost, or Holy Spirit, are one God, co-equal, inseparable, and indivisible. The opposing conclusion may be due to a serious misunderstanding, rather than a detraction. God is the Judge and knows man's heart. Differences in functions does not equate subordination. The Holy Bible neither corroborates nor substantiates the subordination concept or theory.

THE WORK OF THE HOLY SPIRIT IN THE CHURCH

During this presentation, we have seen with our mind's eye the divine work and activities as they relate to the individual believer. We will now consider the work of the Holy Spirit in the church, the Body of Christ, corporately.

The Holy Spirit is the promised gift (Luke 24:49) sent from the Father to indwell believers and to be everything to the church that Jesus would be if he were still here in this earth realm. Jesus commanded the disciples in Matthew 28:18–19 to make other disciples and to teach them to do everything he commanded. Jesus said, "And these signs shall follow them that believe; in my name shall they cast out devils; they shall speak with new tongues; They shall take up serpents; and if they drink any deadly thing, it shall not hurt them; they shall lay hands on the sick, and they shall recover" (Mark 16:17–18).

Christ had power and authority through his relationship with the Father. He pleased the Father; he obeyed the Father; and he spoke only that which he heard the Father speak. He knew his identity and commission as the Son, sent from the Father. (See John 17:2.) Jesus received power through the anointing of the Holy Spirit. (See Luke 4:1, 14, 18.) The prophecy in Isaiah, chapter sixty-one, reads in part: "The Spirit of the Lord GOD is upon me, because he has anointed me to preach good tidings unto the meek."

The believer has been commissioned to minister in power under the authority of Jesus. He dispensed power to his apostles. Jesus promised this power to all believers through the Holy Spirit. We, too, exercise this power out of our position and relationship. Being adopted into God's family, we have all the rights of a child of God by being submissive to our Father. We exercise this power also out of our relationship to Jesus, we being the branches of the Vine. (See John 15:5.) And, finally, we exercise this power out of anointing by the Holy Spirit for service.

This brings us to the question: How does the believer receive this anointing and power to do the greater works that Jesus said the church would do? (See John 14:12.) First of all, John the Baptist prophesied it of Jesus, and Jesus spoke this, himself. It is recorded in all four gospels and the book of Acts that Jesus would "baptize you with the Holy Ghost"; the gospel of Matthew and Luke include "and with fire." (See Matt. 3:11; Mark 1:8; Luke 3:16; John 1:33; Acts 1:3–8.) Only believers can be baptized with the Holy Ghost. The Spirit is already in the believer by the new birth. We are born again of water and of the Spirit. And Jesus said, "That which is born of the flesh is flesh; and that which is born of the Spirit is spirit" (John 3:6). It is written also that "the natural man receives not the things of the Spirit of God;" (1 Cor. 2:14) and, "we have received, not the spirit of the world, but the spirit which is of God; that we might know the things that are freely given to us of God" (1 Cor. 2:12).

After his passion and just before his ascension, Jesus was seen by his disciples for forty days speaking of things pertaining to the kingdom of God. "And being assembled together with them, commanded they that they should not depart from Jerusalem, but wait for the promise of the Father, which saith he, ye have heard of me. For John truly baptized with water; but ye shall be baptized with the Holy Ghost not many days hence. But ye shall receive power, after that the Holy Ghost is come upon you: and ye shall be witnesses unto me" (Acts 1:3–5, 8). The complete account is in Acts 1:3–8. The "not many days hence" that Jesus spoke of came after Passover on the day of Pentecost (Pentecost meaning fiftieth), a day to rejoice before the Lord.

> And so when the day of Pentecost was fully come, they were all with one accord in one place. And suddenly there came a sound from heaven as of a rushing mighty wind, and it filled all the house where they were sitting. And there appeared unto them cloven tongues like fire, and it sat upon each of them. And they were all filled with the Holy Ghost, and began to speak with other tongues, as the Spirit gave them utterance. And there were dwelling at Jerusalem Jews, devout men, out of every nation under heaven. Now

when this was noised abroad, the multitude came together, and were confounded, because that every man heard them speak in his own language. And they were all amazed and marveled, saying one to another, Behold, are not all these which speak Galileans? And how hear we every man in our own tongue, wherin we were born? (Acts 2:1–8).

Pentecostal believers understand from Scripture and from experience that speaking in tongues is the uniform, universal, initial, outward, or physical evidence of having received the baptism of the Holy Ghost. The Spirit baptism is not the same experience as that of being filled with the Spirit received at the new birth or regeneration. They are two separate experiences, and the baptism of the Holy Spirit can occur at any time after the new birth. The evidence of having been baptized by Jesus with the Holy Ghost is that the believer speaks in tongues.

Besides speaking in tongues, the baptism of the Holy Spirit gives the believer access into a new measure of personal holiness, as the believer is sanctified by the Holy Ghost. The office work of the Spirit is to be the personal channel to convey the mind and attitudes of Jesus Christ into the heart and life of the believer. The baptized believer enjoys deeper, richer revelation of the Word of God. He receives power to speak boldly, power to witness, has a passion for souls, new impetus for prayer, a new life of worship and praise, and much more. And the fruit of the Spirit (love, joy, peace, long-suffering, gentleness, goodness, faith, meekness, and temperance) becomes a very real channel to the believer to reproduce his gracious virtues in an abiding submissive relationship to the Spirit. The manifestation of the fruit is rooted in the acts of the Spirit and not in the believer's conscious efforts to bear fruit.

HOW TO RECEIVE THE BAPTISM OF THE HOLY GHOST

Jesus is the baptizer. Jesus baptizes believers with the Holy Ghost. Man baptizes believers in water. Jesus' baptism is associated with the believer's experience in relation to the Holy Ghost. The believer may receive this gift by desiring it and praying for it. The baptism of the Spirit is received by faith, just as salvation is received by faith. The believer yields himself to the unhindered operation of the Spirit so that he is motivated and completely controlled by the Spirit beyond himself. The Holy Spirit anoints the believer with himself to bestow his own person and presence within the believer. The person receiving the baptism of the Spirit will experience a saturation of his inner being by the divine Spirit, and there will be an utterance by the recipient in a language not previously known, or, in other tongues. The Spirit comes to the person when he is invited. The Holy Spirit gives, manifests, and reveals other spiritual gifts to the body of Christ.

THE GIFTS OF THE SPIRIT

The supernatural gifts of the Spirit assist and expand the work of the church in fulfilling its tasks.

Numerous accounts of the manifestations of the gifts of the Spirit had been recorded into the middle of the third century. Afterward, references to these occurrences became less frequent; however, some manifestations were retained. What little doctrine the church had developed on spiritual gifts and miracles had severely degenerated. Any systematic effort to study the gifts of the Spirit had traditionally been discouraged. By the time of the Reformation, the doctrine of miracles in the church had degenerated into virtually animistic superstition. Reformers concluded that the age of miracles was past.

The Pentecostal experience barely survived into the Modern Era. After rejection by the Catholic Church, except for outward ritual, the Protestant reformation began. Throughout the eighteenth century, redevelopment of Pentecostalism began in many parts of the world by leaders and founders. In the nineteenth and twentieth centuries, Spirit baptism and revival was transmitted to various churches and denominations, groups, and colleges by leaders and founders in different parts of the world.

In 1906–1908, there was a great outpouring and revival of the Spirit baptism and manifestations of the gifts of the Spirit at the Azusa Mission of Los Angeles, and it served as a center in which numerous future Pentecostal leaders received their Pentecostal baptismal experience. The results of this revival are highly visible today; however, I believe, as do many other Christians, that the greatest revival and manifestation of the sons of God is on the horizon.

The nine spiritual gifts given by the Spirit are listed in 1 Corinthians 12:4–10 as follows:

- The word of wisdom: It is the special ability given by God to receive instant insight on how a revelation may be applied to a specific situation or need in the body of Christ.
- The word of knowledge: This gift is concerned with the immediate awareness of facts without the aid of the senses. It is supernatural revelation by the Holy Spirit of certain facts in the mind of God.
- Faith: The gift of faith is a supernatural endowment by the Spirit whereby that which is uttered or desired by man, or spoken by God, shall eventually come to pass.
- Gifts of healing: The miraculous manifestation of the Spirit for the banishment of all human ills whether organic, functional, acute, or chronic.
- Working of miracles: A supernatural act; a temporary suspension of the accustomed order; an intervention into the course of nature as it is normally understood.
- Prophecy: The special ability to receive and communicate an immediate message of God to his gathered people, a group among them or any one of his people individually, through divinely anointed utterance.
- Discerning of spirits: This supernatural gift of perception, given sovereignly by God, enables individuals in the church to distinguish the motivating spirit behind certain words or deeds.
- Tongues: Speaking in tongues or praying in the Spirit is what happens when a Christian believer allows the indwelling Spirit to guide the form of words he utters. Tongues are a medium of prayer and worship and of edification. Tongues are a sign. Praying in tongues stimulates faith.

- Interpretation of tongues: A supernatural revelation through the Holy Spirit which enables the Christian believer to communicate in the language of the listeners the dynamic equivalent of that which was spoken in tongues.

Power must never be used without authority. There must be a revelation from God, and we must try to ascertain the Father's will before we use the power. We are instructed to desire spiritual gifts and to covet to prophesy. Manifestation of signs and wonders should be desired for the glory of God and his kingdom and for the benefit of the recipient, not for pride or other carnal reasons. The absence of love will annul the gifts in the believer. It is necessary for the believer to be completely emptied of self and totally dependent upon the Holy Spirit, as this is the degree to which he is empowered by the Spirit.

The gifts of the Spirit operate in conjunction with the ministering gifts given by Jesus when "he ascended up on high." Ephesians 4:11–12 state: "And he gave some, apostles, and some, prophets; and some, evangelists; and some, pastors and teachers; for the perfecting of the saints, for the work of the ministry, for the edifying of the body of Christ."

The church is called to be God's army, continually assaulting the powers of Satan and extending the rule of God. Jesus' ministry of signs and wonders is fundamental to the preaching of the kingdom of God. All of Christ's disciples are given both the authority and power to preach, heal and cast out demons. As this is done the domain of the evil one is driven back and the kingdom of God is advanced. "For the weapons of our warfare are not carnal, but mighty through God to the pulling down of strongholds" (2 Cor. 10:4).

PRAYING IN THE SPIRIT

This brings us to our conclusion. I want to talk briefly about prayer. It is the last part of our discussion but is far from the least.

Prayer is most essential. It is as necessary as breathing. It involves every atom of our being. Praise and thanksgiving are the very life of prayer.

Our prayer life is what we are, just as nutritionists say our physical body is what we eat. Prayer is to be first and predominant in the church and in our individual lives. "It is written, My house is the house of prayer" (Luke 19:46).

Prayer is the surrendering of our whole being to God. The Word of God tells us to: Pray without ceasing; pray for all men everywhere; pray according to the will of God; pray in faith believing. The Spirit baptized believer is encouraged to pray with the spirit and pray with the understanding also. Paul reminds us that we as a church are to be "praying always with all prayer and supplication in the Spirit for all saints." Jude counsels us: "But ye, beloved, building up yourselves on your most holy faith, praying in the Holy Ghost" (verse 20).

The Holy Spirit is our intercessor. We pray to the Father in the name of Jesus and the Holy Spirit intercedes. Romans 8:26 says,

> Likewise the Spirit also helpeth our infirmities: for we know not what we should pray for as we ought: but the Spirit itself maketh intercession for us with groanings which cannot be uttered. And he that searcheth the hearts knoweth what is the mind of the Spirit, because he maketh intercession for the saints according to the will of God.

The Holy Spirit is our communicator—believer to God—God to believer. "For what man knoweth the things of man, save the spirit of man which is in him? Even so the things of God knoweth no man, but the Spirit of God." As believers, "Now we have received, not the spirit of the world, but the spirit which is of God; that we might know the things that are freely given to us of God" (1 Cor. 2:11–12). The apostle John wrote: "He [the Holy Ghost] shall not speak of himself; but whatsoever he shall hear, that shall he speak" (John 16:13).

We can see here the cooperative work of the Trinity and the activity of the Holy Spirit in particular in relation to our communication with the Father. Praying in the spirit is most effective. The Scriptures reveal: "If I pray in an unknown tongue, my spirit prayeth, but my understanding is unfruitful" (1 Cor. 14:14). Prayer is a miracle of the Spirit. Without the

Spirit, no prayer; and without prayer, no Spirit. The believer goes to God through the Spirit. Please keep in mind that through tongues, prayer, and worship are raised to their highest level and elevated far above superficial lip service. "He that speaketh in an unknown tongue speaketh not unto men, but unto God" (1 Cor. 12; 14:2). Amen.

Thank you for being so kind and attentive. I would like to recommend for your reading two books: *The Holy Spirit,* by L. Thomas Holdcroft; and *Spiritual Gifts in the Local Church* by David Pytches.

Appendix B

THE PERFECT WORD OF TRUTH

This appendix gives guidelines to what should inspire an exhaustive undertaking to read, study, hear, understand, and perform the entire word of God.

From eternity to eternity, the Word of God lives. The psalmist declared "thou has magnified thy word above all thy name" (Ps. 138:2). God's sacred name(s) appear in all of Scripture, especially the Old Testament. God's name is holy, hallowed (pure, sanctified, consecrated). His name is to be revered and feared above all names. We understand, therefore, that God's Word transcends all that his holy name conveys.

"In the beginning was the Word," Jesus. The Word was God. The worlds were framed by the Word of God. Jesus is the Light of the world that shined out of darkness to give light (understanding) and the knowledge of God.

From the first word of Genesis to the last word of Revelation, God reveals his eternal truths, intentions, and purposes for the benefit of mankind. In these last days, Jesus has ordained, anointed, and gifted teachers with the ability to receive and comprehend profound knowledge and revelation of the Word. They teach the entire church the entire undivided Word of knowledge and counsel. Comprehensive biblical teaching reveals, instructs, admonishes, enlightens, and empowers those who seek truth.

God manifests hidden meanings of his divine actions. Christians who diligently seek God, through a profusion of effectual prayer and study of every word, will be in readiness to gain extraordinary perception of past, present, and future truths, including prophecies and mysteries in Revelation. God's Word is powerful, alive, and pervasive, dividing soul from spirit and joints from marrow. It discerns and searches the thoughts and intents of the heart.

God counsels believers to let the Word of God dwell in them richly. The prophet Hosea spoke these words from God: "My people are destroyed for lack of knowledge: because thou has rejected knowledge" (Hos. 4:6). The prophet Amos wrote: "Behold, the days come, saith the Lord GOD, that I will send a famine in the land, not a famine of bread, nor a thirst for water, but of hearing the words of the LORD" (Amos 8:11). Jesus speaks holy words of spirit and life. The Word of God is neither interpreted nor understood by natural means. The Spirit residing in believers reveals the Word to those who listen. "In the beginning God said" (spoke). Jesus is revealed throughout Scripture, as he is the Word. The redeemed of God are also portrayed in the Word. God chose believers in Christ before the foundation of the world. In the world they were born first of the flesh and born again of the Spirit, of incorruptible seed, the Word of God.

Jesus, the Word, spoke: "I come (in the volume of the book it is written of me) to do thy will, O God." At the appointed time, God sent his written word, the Bible, to the world through scrolls, translations, and printing press. The Bible was written by holy men of God as they were moved by the Holy Ghost. There were approximately forty chosen writers. Thirty wrote the Old Testament and ten wrote the New Testament.

The Word is to be experienced. "O taste and see that the LORD is good" (Ps. 34:8). "How sweet are thy words unto my taste! yea, sweeter than honey to my mouth!" (Ps. 119:103). "The entrance of thy words gives light" (Ps. 119:130). "As the rain cometh down, . . . from heaven . . . that it may give seed . . . and bread . . . So shall my word be that goeth forth out of my mouth: it shall not return unto me void, but it shall accomplish that which I please, and it shall prosper in the thing whereto I sent it," (Isa. 55:10–11) saith the Lord.

OLD TESTAMENT

The Old Testament records the beginnings of God's operations and actions, covering about four thousand years of original interactions between God and his creation. The Word affords the people of God the privilege of knowing why and how God commanded certain actions according to the extent of his disclosure to us. God's grace, blessings, and forgiveness and man's responses, with consequences and final outcomes, were unceasing. This period of time encompasses the past, present, and future of mankind and the world, including a glimpse of the blessed hope of eternity. An abbreviated narration of events and actions of God and reactions of man is provided merely as a framework for meticulous thorough study of every word of God.

The thirty-nine books of the Old Testament incorporate the beginnings and history of all peoples and nations of the world. The apparent focus and attention given almost exclusively to the nation of Israel, the Jews, throughout the Old Testament, is clarified soon after the end of the great flood. The purpose of God's selectivity would soon be revealed in God's extraordinary action of total inclusion of all mankind, without exception. Through Abraham, God's grace provides justification by faith to everyone, without respect of any person.

The Old Testament reveals God's divine order as shown in the account of six days of creation and follows with great and mighty acts.

- First day: Light (day); Darkness (night).
- Second day: Heaven (firmament above waters).
- Third day: Earth (waters under heaven gathered together, dry land appears).
- Fourth day: Sun, Moon, Stars.
- Fifth day: Living creatures (birds, winged fowls, whales, creatures in waters).
- Sixth day: Man (Male, Female); God made Adam in his image from the dust of the ground.
- God revealed the Seed of salvation (Jesus).

- The fall of Adam (man).
- Both salvation and condemnation of man demonstrated in Noah and the flood.
- Salvation by the faith of Abraham established.
- Test and result of faith symbolically shown in the sacrifice of Isaac and substitution of the lamb.
- Jacob's name changed to Israel; birth of the nation.
- Israeli nation, population of seventy, moves to Egypt, saved from famine by Joseph, Jacob's son.
- The nation, Israel, is proved for forty years in Egypt.
- Moses, God's chosen deliverer, rescues Israel from Egyptian bondage.
- Forty years of wilderness wanderings; the law is given; tabernacle is built.
- Joshua leads Israel back to promised land; their transgressions against God continue.
- Troubled by hostile nations, they implore God, who appoints judges to judge and to lead in fighting their battles.
- Discontented Israel asked God to appoint a king over them like other nations.
- God answered and appoints Saul as king, who proved to be their undoing.
- God chooses and anoints David to be king of Israel, forerunner of the King of Kings and Lord of Lords, Jesus Christ.
- As warned and prophesied, Israel is divided into two kingdoms, Israel and Judah.
- Prophets prophesy to both nations of their impending seventy years of captivity in Babylon.
- After seventy years, return to Jerusalem from Babylonian captivity.
- Approximately four hundred years ensue before the coming of Christ, the Messiah.
- The word of the Lord through Malachi: God reminds Israel of their sins and of his love for them. He prophesied that God would send his messenger, John the Baptist, to prepare the way of the Lord.
- An approximate four-hundred-year interval before Christ.

The foregoing outline enables searchers of Scripture to remember very easily which primary events and related principal persons are found in which books of the Bible. This makes it extremely feasible to understand the importance and purpose of vital truths of the Old Covenant that precede as well as embody the New Testament.

NEW TESTAMENT

Of the twenty-seven books of the New Testament, two of the four gospels and twenty epistles were written by apostles. There are differing origins or accounts and uncertainties about the authorship of Acts and Hebrews. The Scriptures show that the continuity from the Old Testament to the New Testament is of the administration of the Spirit of the Lord. The faith of Abraham and the law as schoolmaster brought about freedom from the law of sin and death. Righteousness that is of God is by faith. Souls are transformed by the Spirit of the Lord, the end of the Old Testament letter of the law. Throughout their history, Israelites struggled with sin and idolatry, for the ways of righteousness and holiness were not fully known until Christ's sacrifice. Jesus, the living Word, speaks in spirit, in truth, and in person. On one occasion, he reminded his disciples: "All things must be fulfilled, which were written in the law of Moses, and in the prophets, and in the psalms, concerning me" (Luke 24:44). Jesus, the Word, is Alpha (the beginning, Genesis) and Omega (the ending, Revelation).

The New Testament records two of three distinct, major delineations of the Bible. The second is the glorious fulfillment of the promise of the coming of Jesus Christ, the Son of God, the Messiah, and Son of Man. Prophecies came to pass with Jesus' humble birth, cruel death, his resurrection, earthly mission, and return to the Father. The third division involves the revelation of a multitude of drastic and intensely powerful actions preceding the end of this present age, the end of time, the creation of a new heaven and a new earth, and the coming of the kingdom of heaven. The Bible declares, "The end of all things is at hand" (1 Peter 4:7). And Jesus says, "Behold, I make all things new" (Rev. 1:5).

New Testament writings for these last days begin with disclosure of the genealogy of Jesus. The gospel of Matthew lists the ancestry and lineage of Jesus, beginning with Abraham and extending to King David, spanning fourteen generations. From David until the Babylonian captivity were fourteen generations, and from that period to the birth of Christ were fourteen generations. Luke also documents the genealogy of Christ in reverse chronology.

Each writer of the four gospels gives their own account of the ministry and works of Jesus from birth to the end of his earthly mission. Significantly, the twelve apostles were eyewitnesses, personally chosen, taught and trained by Jesus. He commissioned, anointed, and fully prepared apostles and prophets to be a part of the foundation with him of the church which was to come.

In the beginning of his ministry, Jesus proceeded to convert the Jews by proclaiming to them that he was the One, their Messiah, who had come in the flesh in fulfillment of prophecy. The Gentiles were not excluded, as Jesus performed miracles for all to see and preached repentance, the kingdom of heaven, and eternal salvation to all. John the Baptist not only announced the coming of Jesus but also the coming of the Holy Ghost to the church and to the world. All four gospels recorded and announced that Jesus would baptize believers with the Holy Ghost after his return to the Father.

Acts records the last words of instruction Jesus gave to his disciples before ascending to heaven; the coming of the Holy Ghost to the church and the world; the birth of the church, its succeeding victories as well as severe opposition and challenges of adversaries; and the spread of Christianity from Jerusalem to the utmost parts of the world.

The epistles are written to churches, believers, individuals, and doubting Jewish believers. Hebrews, along with Galatians and Romans, explain and extol the validity and superiority of faith and grace through Jesus Christ as opposed to the former law and ordinances that some Jews were reluctant to abandon. Apostles' letters extensively teach and affirm the faith and doctrinal truths. They inspire, encourage, inform, admonish, discipline, as well as reinforce ethical and moral principles relative to personal behavior. Disciples are warned and counseled regarding enemies of the faith. Apostles are responsible to establish local churches to operate according to the Word of God in every detail. Church success, growth and prosperity is measured, biblically, by the extent of believers' spiritual maturity and by their work in the ministry, not by their attendance or financial capabilities. Words of the prophets from God exhort, maintain statute, discipline, integrity, and order in the church. Timely words keep the church on the right course. Teachers are anointed and endued with exceptional biblical knowledge to teach the entire church profound truths. In his wisdom, God placed apostles, prophets, and teachers in the church in that order for its good and God's eternal purposes.

A partial profile of the New Testament is offered to encourage thorough search and study:

- John the Baptist announces the coming of Jesus.
- Jesus is born.
- Jesus preaches repentance and the kingdom of heaven to the Jews.
- Jesus offers salvation also to Gentiles.
- Jesus chooses, anoints, ordains, and empowers twelve apostles for ministry.
- Jesus prepares the disciples for his crucifixion, resurrection, and ascension.
- The crucifixion.
- The resurrection.
- Jesus' final instructions to his disciples and followers.
- The ascension.
- Coming of the Holy Spirit.
- The church is born and established by the apostles and prophets.
- Christianity grows and expands.
- Letters from Apostle Paul repeatedly distinguish for the Jews the difference between law and grace.
- Apostles and disciples travel to many cities and towns appointing and confirming church leaders and establishing churches in true doctrine.
- The writings of Apostles James, Peter, John, and Jude also thoroughly expound the Word of God to edify, exhort, and comfort.

- All apostles give complete instructions to the church to cover every aspect of believers' behavior. This includes their relationship to God and their conduct toward spouse, children, other believers, and all peoples in all circumstances.

The third and final segment of the perceived divisions in the New Testament concerns the Revelation of God to the church for these last days. The whole world continues to experience perplexing events prophesied especially in Revelation but also in the gospels and other books of the Bible. We are told in Revelation: Blessed is he that reads, hears, and keeps the words of this prophecy, for the time is at hand. (See Rev. 1:3.) Believers have the blessed privilege of understanding current happenings and discerning those prophecies yet to be fulfilled accordingly as we desire and God wills. In the gospels, Jesus warns of perils, catastrophes, wars, distress of nations, wickedness, loss of love, and many more adversities. In Revelation, Jesus exhorts and instructs the seven churches in Asia. The church of today should also be mindful that the first thing Jesus did was to show his abiding love by cautioning them to get their house in order. He exhorted these churches to overcome, a necessity for believers to receive rewards and to rule with him in his glorious eternal reign.

When we read Revelation, we should be alerted to know when the seven seals are opened, when the seven trumpets are sounded, and when the seven vials are poured out in the earth. For instance, from seals being opened, we see already such things as peace being taken from the earth so that men kill one another; equity is far out of balance; oil problems persist. It is recorded that the church shall be severely persecuted by the serpent and some are martyred. Jesus and the saints shall victoriously overcome and defeat the devil. To the contrary, unbelievers worship the beast and his image, who performs great miracles. He exerts great power, and demands that his worshippers receive his mark or his number (666) in their right hand or forehead or be killed. These are only a sampling of a great array of the most drastic events known to man.

At the appointed time, it shall come to pass that the old shall pass and the new shall begin. Jesus and the saints, eventually, shall judge angels, and judge the world with the fierceness and wrath of Almighty God, with a rod of iron broken to shivers. (See Rev. 2:27; 19:15.) Jesus says that he will give power over the nations to believers who keep his works to the end. Believers should be eternally grateful, because Jesus shows us his abiding love and care by warning us, individually and collectively, to set in order the things that are lacking. These times definitely signify the soon coming of Jesus. He says to the children of God: "Let not your heart be troubled: . . . I go to prepare a place for you . . . I will come again and receive you unto myself" (John 14:1–3). It is high time to be vigilant and to prepare the way of the Lord. Jesus alerts us: "When ye see these things [as have been mentioned] come to pass, know ye that the kingdom of God is nigh at hand" (Luke 21:31). The answer to thousands of years of believers praying: "Thy kingdom come" is near (Matt. 6:10). The sounding of the seventh trumpet signals: "The kingdoms of this world are become the kingdoms of our Lord and of his Christ" (Rev. 11:15). Also, a voice in heaven proclaimed: "Now is come . . . the kingdom of our God and the power of his Christ"(Rev. 12:10). Jesus says, "Surely I come quickly" (Rev. 22:20).

Writing this agenda and the entire book is with humble gratitude. It is the burden of the Lord to the church urging church renewal grounded in the entire Word of Truth. The grace of our Lord Jesus Christ be with you all. Amen.

ABOUT THE AUTHOR

Rubye Edwards was raised in Atlanta, Georgia and was the second of eight children. She remembers the hardships of the Great Depression of the 1930s. As was common during that time, her family lived on meager means.

In spite of this, upon her graduation from high school, Edwards enrolled in Reid's Business College. She acquired secretarial and bookkeeping skills and graduated with honors. Upon moving to Washington DC, Edwards utilized those skills as she began her career as a government employee serving in several federal agencies.

Her first employment was as a secretary in the U.S. Department of State, Far East Division. In the Department of State, Edwards had the distinct honor of being selected to serve on the secretarial staff at the Japanese Peace Treaty Conference, held in 1951 in San Francisco, California. In 1952, Edwards received a two-year secretarial assignment at the U.S. Embassy in Tokyo, Japan. While in Japan, Edwards attended Sophia University, and completed about two years of basic academic credits with honors.

With her return to the states, Edwards resided in Chicago, Illinois and was employed as a secretary with the Department of Health, Education, and Welfare. It was in Chicago where Edwards's life was transformed through her renewed commitment to God as the preeminent One in her life. A deep interest in the Word of God led her to enroll in Moody Bible Institute. From that time forward, she became engrossed in Bible study and devoted to prayer.

After her retirement and the death of her son, Edwards moved back to Georgia where she currently resides.